D1553851

WITNESS *for* HIS NAMES

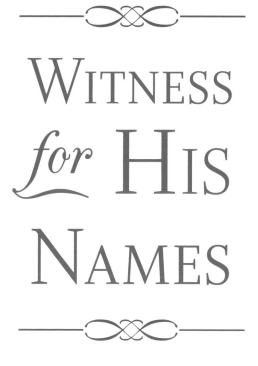

WITNESS
for HIS
NAMES

JEFFREY R. HOLLAND

DESERET
BOOK

Salt Lake City, Utah

Interior images: Shutterstock.com

Visit us at deseretbook.com

Library of Congress Cataloging-in-Publication Data
(CIP data on file)
ISBN 978-1-62972-709-7

Printed in China
RR Donnelley, Dongguan, China
10   9   8   7   6   5   4   3   2   1

For Pat

WHO KNOWS HIS NAME
AND KNOWS HIM

WHEREFORE GOD ALSO HATH HIGHLY EXALTED HIM,

AND GIVEN HIM A NAME WHICH IS ABOVE EVERY NAME:

THAT AT THE NAME OF JESUS EVERY KNEE SHOULD BOW...

AND... EVERY TONGUE SHOULD CONFESS THAT

JESUS CHRIST IS LORD

—PHILIPPIANS 2:9–11

NO SWEETER SOUND THAN
THY BLESSED NAME

This year marks my twenty-fifth year as a member of the Quorum of the Twelve Apostles of The Church of Jesus Christ of Latter-day Saints. Through the very challenging nights and wonderfully rewarding days of that calling, I have tried to feel equal to the responsibilities inherent in such a sacred office. At the same time, I have tried *not* to feel overwhelmed by the sense of inadequacy that never seems to abate. After two and a half decades, I haven't made much progress toward either goal. My apostolic calling is still the same unspeakable privilege and humbling obligation I felt it to be on the twenty-third of June, 1994.

With a great desire to be honorable from the first day on, I threw myself into reading all I could about the holy apostleship. I read in the scriptures, I read biblical essays and commentaries, and I read the sermons of those who have so served. Amidst all else I was coming to know early in my study, I learned that among the most important responsibilities I had was to be one of the "special witnesses of the name of Christ in all the world—[and] . . . to officiate in the name of the Lord, . . . agreeable to the institution of heaven" (Doctrine and Covenants 107:23, 33). There was more:

"Behold, Jesus Christ is the *name* which is given of the Father, and there is none other *name* given whereby man can be saved;

"Wherefore, all men must take upon them the *name* which is given of the Father, for in that *name* shall they be called at the last day;

"Wherefore, if they know not the *name* by which they are called, they cannot have place in the kingdom of my Father.

"And now, behold, there are others who are called to declare my gospel, both unto Gentile and unto Jew;

"Yea, even twelve; and the Twelve shall be my disciples, and they shall take upon them my *name;* and the Twelve are they who shall desire to take upon them my *name* with full purpose of heart.

"And if they desire to take upon them my *name* with full purpose of heart, they are called to go into all the world to preach my gospel unto every creature" (Doctrine and Covenants 18:23–28; emphasis added).

I didn't grasp all that that meant, but it was obvious the *name* of Christ was central to these scriptural mandates and it would require "full purpose of heart" to fulfill them successfully.

All of this carried with it an echo from my youth, when I first became aware that so many things (all covenantal things) done in the Church were done in the *name* of Deity.

I remembered from my own baptism as well as those I

performed as a missionary that this sacred ordinance was to be performed "in the name of the Father, and of the Son, and of the Holy Ghost" (Doctrine and Covenants 20:73).

I remembered that taking the sacrament of the Lord's Supper, or passing it, or blessing it, involved a prayer in which we asked God "in the name of [the] Son" for blessings that could come only to those who were "willing to take upon them the name of thy Son" (Doctrine and Covenants 20:77).

Every other ordinance I had experienced in my youth, including my patriarchal blessing, my ordination to various priesthood offices, assorted blessings and settings apart, and the majesty of the entire temple experience were all administered either in the name of Jesus Christ or in the name of the Father, and of the Son, and of the Holy Ghost.

That history coupled with this new calling led to a habit in my daily scripture study of jotting down or otherwise noting the references to Jesus's various names that I found in the standard works.

As my study continued rather casually over the years, I was greatly blessed when my apostolic brother, Elder Dallin Oaks—then of the Quorum of the Twelve Apostles, now of the First Presidency—published a mind-expanding and Apostle-educating little book entitled *His Holy Name*. It remains the definitive work on the many uses to which the name of Christ can be put, suggesting the doctrine and significance of names generally and the name of Christ specifically. He reflected on the wide variety of purposes—well beyond simple identification—for which the name of Christ can be invoked. Because these purposes provide a valuable backdrop to the work I have done, I share the essence of them here.

NAME AS AUTHORITY OR PRIESTHOOD OR POWER

Example: Peter and John invoked the name of Jesus in healing the lame man at the temple in Jerusalem. In that encounter, Peter said, "In the *name* of Jesus Christ of Nazareth rise up and walk" (Acts 3:6; emphasis added). When the man was instantly healed, Peter explained to the stunned onlookers: "And his *name* through faith in his *name* hath made this man strong" (Acts 3:16; emphasis added). (Joseph Smith's inspired translation of the Bible makes this verse clearer and easier to understand: "And this man, through faith in his name, hath been made strong.") Later, when Peter and John were arrested, their captors asked, "By what power, or by what *name*, have ye done this?" Peter replied, "By the *name* of Jesus Christ of Nazareth" (Acts 4:7, 10; emphasis added).

NAME AS WORK OR PLAN

Example: The work of the Atonement is characterized as being inextricably linked with Christ's name: "And behold, it is he that cometh to take away the sins of the world, yea, the sins of every man who steadfastly believeth on his *name*" (Alma 5:48; emphasis added). Again, "And he shall come into the world to redeem his people; and he shall take upon him the transgressions of those who believe on his *name*; and these are they that shall have eternal life, and salvation cometh to none else" (Alma 11:40; emphasis added). This redemptive plan, carried forward in Christ's name, leads directly to the temple: "Verily I say unto you, it is expedient in me that the first elders of my church should receive their endowment from on high in my house, which I have commanded to be built unto my *name* in the land of Kirtland" (Doctrine and Covenants 105:33; emphasis added).

NAME AS ESSENCE OR EXALTATION

Example: In response to God instructing Moses to lead the children of Israel out of Egypt, Moses replied, "Behold, when I come unto the children of Israel, and shall say unto them, The God of your fathers hath sent me unto you; and they shall say to me, What is his name? what shall I say unto them? And God said unto Moses, I AM THAT I AM: and he said, Thus shalt thou say unto the children of Israel, I AM hath sent me unto you" (Exodus 3:13–14). When Moses was asking to know the name of God, or at least how to identify Him to Pharaoh, he was asking to know the essence or the nature of God. The answer he got was in the first-person present tense of the verb "to be." The answer was given in terms of God's ever-present essence.

Elder Oaks's work, to which the brief examples above do not do adequate justice, gave me increased awareness of the meanings a name can carry. It also quickened in me equal parts of zeal and anxiety to know *how many name(s) of Christ there actually were.* *Jesus* I knew, and *Christ* I knew, and of course a few others—*Savior, Redeemer, Lord*—but I was coming to understand that in order to do my duty to bear witness of His name, officiate in it, and comprehend in more detail the wide variety of functions it informed, I needed to identify those names and think more about them and what they meant regarding Jesus's mission. This feeling grew within me until I came to understand I was dealing with something very significant, doctrinally speaking, and something very large. It didn't take long to feel overwhelmed with the majestic labels, titles, and designations for this Only Perfect Being who ever lived in mortality. The *name of Christ* was growing and swelling, expanding and emerging into the *names of Christ.*

More recently my interest in these many facets of Christ's life and ministry, as revealed in various titles, came to a head. I felt a strong impression to collect my notes and give some order to my thoughts as part of the testimony of Jesus Christ I would leave to my children and grandchildren after I am gone. I had been moving along on that task when I received added, new incentive from President Russell M. Nelson, then the President of the Quorum of the Twelve Apostles. In a worldwide devotional broadcast to young adults, this gifted scholar of the scriptures in his own right counseled these young people to "study everything Jesus Christ *is* by prayerfully and vigorously seeking to understand what each of His various titles and names means *personally* for you" ("Prophets, Leadership, and Divine Law," January 8, 2017; emphasis in original).

Thus, the prompting I had received years ago to put some of my thoughts down on paper became a more intense labor of love as I not only followed this spiritual direction given to me from heaven above but also obeyed the counsel of my quorum president who would within a year become the President of the Church. As fully as my busy schedule would allow, I intensified my study of the wonderfully broad range of Christ's titles and designations.

These names by which Jesus Christ is variously known through His premortal, mortal, and postmortal ministry are not only the focal point of this book, they are the only point of this book. The entire manuscript is devoted to just One Person and how His distinctive characteristics, His virtues, qualities, and accomplishments, affect all who make covenant with Him. The marvelous thing about all of this is that through His glorious Atonement and Resurrection, Christ gives us rebirth and becomes the father of our eternal life. Thus, we speak of being "born again" as sons and daughters of Christ (see John 3:3; Mosiah 5:7), and if we make this conversion thorough enough, Jesus's identity becomes, at least in part, *our* identity both in time and in eternity (see 1 John 3:2–3; Moroni 7:48). As we study these titles to learn more about who He was and is, we will find ourselves learning more about who we are and what we may become.

It should be noted that I have *not* included in this study the many descriptions of Jesus's character or personality unless at some point such a description became an actual title for Him. For example, if one of the verses described Christ as humble and meek—and many did—I did *not* include those in the book unless "Humble" or "Meek" was used as an actual name for Him. Obviously, if I had included all the descriptions of His qualities and virtues without the limitation I imposed, the book would have been much larger than it is.

It is my earnest hope that perhaps one student of the life of Jesus Christ will have her or his testimony of Him strengthened as a result of this modest little book. It has been written in the bright light of true doctrine that declares "there is none other . . . name given under heaven whereby man can be saved in the kingdom of God" (2 Nephi 31:21).

WHOM SAY YE THAT I AM?

In what has come to be called the Great Confession, Jesus asked His disciples walking with Him near the coasts of Cæsarea Philippi who the common men and women of the countryside thought He was. They dutifully answered, "Some say that thou art John the Baptist: some, Elias; and others, Jeremias, or one of the prophets."

He probed further, getting at what was for Him a more important question. "But whom say *ye* that I am?" He asked. That pivotal, penetrating question, the spirit of which will be asked of every man, woman, and child who has ever lived, elicited this great apostolic witness from Peter: "Thou art the Christ, the Son of the living God" (Matthew 16:13–16; emphasis added).

Names are important and have been from the beginning of history. In the great primeval days of creation, the record says:

"And out of the ground I, the Lord God, formed every beast of the field, and every fowl of the air; and commanded that they should come unto Adam, to see what he would call them; and they were also living souls; for I, God, breathed into them the breath of life, and commanded that whatsoever Adam called every living creature, that should be the name thereof.

"And Adam gave names to all cattle, and to the fowl of the air, and to every beast of the field" (Moses 3:19–20).

From that day to this, creating and cataloging the names of things in order to know more precisely what (or who) they are has been a task undertaken by prophets and poets, scholars and scientists in every field of endeavor. "Name it to know it" could well be every taxonomist's motto. It could be that of every disciple of Christ as well.

But however important it may be in the secular world to name the flora and fauna, the beasts of the field and the fowls of the air, it is a much more important tradition in the gospel of Jesus Christ to name *people* and to do so in a way that either identifies one of their principal characteristics (almost always a virtuous one) or offers the motivation to acquire such. Adam and Eve themselves bore names that suggested their roles here in mortality (see Moses 1:34; 4:26), and when important covenants were made, men like Abram, Jacob, and Simon took on new names that signaled a new life as well as a new identity (see Genesis 17:5; 32:28; Matthew 16:18).

In a very motivating albeit somewhat unusual way, the prophet Lehi used names to encourage his wayward sons, Laman and Lemuel. To inspire the former, Lehi named a wilderness river *Laman* in hopes that his son by that name "mightest be like unto this river, continually running into the fountain of all righteousness!" In like manner he named a nearby valley *Lemuel* that this son "mightest be like unto this valley, firm and steadfast, and immovable in keeping the commandments of the Lord!" (1 Nephi 2:8–10, 14).

Later in the Book of Mormon, the prophet Helaman said to his sons Nephi and Lehi:

"Behold, my sons, . . . I have given unto you the names of our first parents who came out of the land of Jerusalem; and this I have done that when you remember your names ye may remember them; and when ye remember them ye may remember their works; and when ye remember their works ye may know how that it is said, and also written, that they were good.

"Therefore, my sons, I would that ye should do that which is good, that it may be said of you, and also written, even as it has been said and written of them" (Helaman 5:6–7).

This preoccupation with—or at least thorough commitment to— noble names is part of our life as well. The naming and blessing of a baby is the first ordinance a child experiences if she or he is fortunate enough to be born to a family that provides such. That name is then used on all the official records of the Church to document that person's progress through the saving ordinances of the Church, on the pedigree charts and family trees that link the human family, and as key words in the holy temple ordinances themselves. If a person is a convert to the Church, it is as Moroni said in Book of Mormon times: He or she is "received unto baptism" and "numbered among the people of the church of Christ; *and their names [are] taken,* that they might be remembered and nourished by the good word of God, to keep them in the right way" (Moroni 6:3–4, emphasis added). At the conclusion of mortal life, we often dedicate a burial site, noting the deceased person by name and inscribing that identity on a marker memorializing his or her final resting place.

Whatever we say of the importance of identity in the mortal world, it gets even more important when applied to matters of the Spirit. In our search "to know . . . God, and Jesus Christ, whom [He] hast sent" (John 17:3), we can learn more about who Christ was, is, and will yet be by examining the names and titles given to Him than by any other method. As the marvelous James E. Talmage wrote: "The divinity of Jesus Christ is indicated by the specific names and titles authoritatively applied to Him. According to man's judgment there may be but little importance attached to names; but in the nomenclature of the Gods every name is a title of power or station" (*Jesus the Christ* [1915], 33).

As in so many matters of Church doctrine, the Book of Mormon helps educate us regarding the "titles of power or station" that Christ received. At the close of King Benjamin's masterful sermon, the people responded in unison to the stunning spiritual experience they had had. Note not only the moral significance that moment held for them but more specifically the centrality the name of Christ would have in the covenant they were making:

"And they all cried with one voice, saying: Yea, we believe all the words which thou hast spoken unto us; and also, we know of their surety and truth, because of the Spirit of the Lord Omnipotent, which has wrought a mighty change in us, or in our hearts, that we have no more disposition to do evil, but to do good continually. . . .

"And we are willing to enter into a covenant with our God to do his will, and to be obedient to his commandments in all things that he shall command us, all the remainder of our days, . . .

"And now, these are the words which king Benjamin desired of them; and therefore he said unto them: Ye have spoken the words that I desired; and the covenant which ye have made is a righteous covenant" (Mosiah 5:2, 5–6).

King Benjamin's response to that moment brought them a new identity, even a new birthright (parentage), that he pronounced upon these reborn people:

"And now, because of the covenant which ye have made ye shall be called the children of Christ, his sons, and his daughters; for behold, this day he hath spiritually begotten you; for ye say that your hearts are changed through faith on his name; therefore, ye are born of him and have become his sons and his daughters.

"And under this head ye are made free, and there is no other head whereby ye can be made free. There is no other name given whereby salvation cometh; therefore, I would that ye should take upon you the name of Christ, all you that have entered into the covenant with God that ye should be obedient unto the end of your lives.

"And it shall come to pass that whosoever doeth this shall be found at the right hand of God, for he shall know the name by which he is called; for he shall be called by the name of Christ.

"And now it shall come to pass, that whosoever shall not take upon him the name of Christ must be called by some other name; therefore, he findeth himself on the left hand of God.

"And I would that ye should remember also, that this is the name that I said I should give unto you that never should be blotted out, except it be through transgression; therefore, take heed that ye do not transgress, that the name be not blotted out of your hearts.

"I say unto you, I would that ye should remember to retain the name written always in your hearts, that ye are not found on the left hand of God, but that ye hear and know the voice by which ye shall be called, and also, the name by which he shall call you" (Mosiah 5:7–12).

Truly, there is "no other name given whereby salvation cometh." May we joyfully take the name of Christ upon us as an indication of the covenant we have made to "be obedient unto the end of [our] lives" (Mosiah 5:8).

NAMES AND

TITLES OF

Jesus Christ

THE LAST
ADAM

Just as Jehovah and Michael acted together under the direction of Elohim in the days of creation, so they performed complementary roles under His direction in mortality as well. Michael became the first Adam, giving us physical life. Jehovah became Jesus, the Last Adam, who gave us eternal life. The Fall of Adam and Eve and the Atonement of Christ were always intended to be taught as complementary parts of a common plan.

ROMANS 5:12–21; 1 CORINTHIANS 15:45

ADONAI

This word means literally "My Lords." It is the plural form of *adon* or *Lord.* It is one of the principal Hebrew synonyms for Jehovah, used in the Hebrew Bible more than 430 times to refer to the Divine Being of the Old Testament, He who would later be born into mortality as Jesus Christ.

ADVOCATE

ADVOCATE WITH THE FATHER

———— ➤•◄ ————

An advocate is one who intercedes for, represents, or pleads the cause of another, particularly in a court of law or at the bar of justice. Jesus is the Advocate with the Father in behalf of all who confess His name and keep His commandments. He is the only one who has lived worthily enough to come into the presence of the Almighty and make the case for the rest of humankind.

1 JOHN 2:1; DOCTRINE AND COVENANTS 29:5; 32:3; 62:1; 110:4

AHMAN

———— ➤•◄ ————

See Son Ahman

Almighty

ALMIGHTY GOD

THE LORD ALMIGHTY

———— ➤•◄ ————

See also Omnipotent; Power

This title refers to the power and might of Jesus, a characteristic He shares with the Father, to whom this title is usually applied (see Advocate with the Father). Christ is almighty (omnipotent) in the sense that He has the complete power and unlimited capability to do everything that can be done. Some things cannot be done even by Deity, such as saving a man in his sins.

GENESIS 17:1; 49:25; 2 CORINTHIANS 6:18; REVELATION 1:8; 4:8; DOCTRINE AND COVENANTS 20:21; 84:118; 109:77; 121:33

ALPHA AND OMEGA

———— ✦ ————

See also First and Last; Beginning and End;
Eternal; Everlasting

THESE ARE THE FIRST AND LAST LETTERS OF THE GREEK ALPHABET. THEIR MEANING IS SYNONYMOUS WITH "THE FIRST AND THE LAST" AND "THE BEGINNING AND THE END," SUGGESTING THE PERMANENT, EVERLASTING, NEVER-FAILING PRESENCE OF JESUS CHRIST IN THE GREAT PLAN OF REDEMPTION, IN HIS TRIUMPH OF LIFE OVER DEATH, IN SALVATION FROM SIN. HE IS OMNIPRESENT, IMMOVABLE, AND VICTORIOUS FROM START TO FINISH IN THE CAUSE OF ETERNAL LIFE. HE IS WITH US THROUGH IT ALL, ALWAYS RELIABLE AND ALWAYS NEARBY.

REVELATION 1:8, 11; 21:6; 22:13; 3 NEPHI 9:18;
DOCTRINE AND COVENANTS 19:1; 35:1; 38:1; 45:7; 54:1; 61:1;
63:60; 68:35; 75:1; 81:7; 84:120; 95:17; 112:34; 132:66

AMEN

This Hebrew word—literally translated as "firm" or "faithful"—means "let it be as has been said." It is most often found as a benediction uttered at the end of a prayer, confirming the words that have been uttered or invoking the fulfillment of them. As such, it is a one-word affirmation of what has been spoken or done or promised. As a title for Jesus Christ, it means that every word He has uttered will be fulfilled and every promise He has made will be kept. Through Him the purposes of God will be firmly and faithfully realized.

REVELATION 3:14; ABRAHAM 3:17

ANGEL

ANGEL OF THE LORD
ANGEL OF HIS PRESENCE

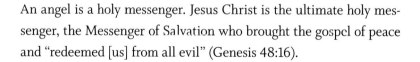

An angel is a holy messenger. Jesus Christ is the ultimate holy messenger, the Messenger of Salvation who brought the gospel of peace and "redeemed [us] from all evil" (Genesis 48:16).

EXODUS 3:2; 23:20–21; ISAIAH 63:9; ACTS 7:30, 35;
DOCTRINE AND COVENANTS 133:52–56

ANOINTED ONE

See also Christ; Messiah

The English word *Christ* comes from a Greek word meaning "anointed" or "the anointed one." That is the same meaning of the Hebrew word *Messiah.* Jesus was anointed by the Father in the premortal world to carry out the Atonement as prescribed in the great plan of salvation. There may have been, as Peter declared, the spirit of an additional anointing following Jesus's baptism at the hands of John: "God anointed Jesus of Nazareth with the Holy Ghost and with power" (Acts 10:38). The significance of an anointing is in the special appointment, function, or privilege it commemorates.

ISAIAH 61:1; LUKE 4:14–21; ACTS 4:27; 10:38; HEBREWS 1:9

APOSTLE

The literal meaning of *Apostle* is "one sent forth." In gospel terms, and as it pertains to a priesthood office, an Apostle is one who is sent with the witness that Jesus is the Christ. Only once is Christ Himself called an Apostle, but He regularly speaks of Himself as being sent from the Father to do the Father's will.

EZEKIEL 2:3; JOHN 5:23, 36, 37; 6:39, 44, 57; 8:16, 18, 29, 42; 10:36; 12:49; 14:24; 17:21, 25; 20:21; HEBREWS 3:1; 1 JOHN 4:14

AUTHOR

AUTHOR OF FAITH

AUTHOR OF SALVATION

A commonly understood definition of *author* is one who writes or creates a work, one who causes something to happen. In this way Christ is the "author of salvation." In an earlier time, the word also meant "prince," "chief leader," or "captain," and is translated as such in some versions of the Bible. This definition means, of course, that Jesus is the first in the company, captain of the faithful. Both of these definitions apply to the plan of salvation and the redeeming faith one must have in the Lord Jesus Christ. He is not only the object of our faith but is also the perfect example of faith. Under the guidance of His Heavenly Father, Christ came to earth to fulfill and give living dimension to the plan for saving all the Father's children. Father and Son authored a masterpiece, whose narrative starts from before the world was and continues into eternity.

HEBREWS 5:9; 12:2; MORONI 6:4

BEGINNING AND END

See Alpha and Omega

ISAIAH 41:4; REVELATION 1:8; 3:14; 21:6; 22:13;
3 NEPHI 9:18; DOCTRINE AND COVENANTS 19:1;
35:1; 38:1; 45:7; 49:12; 54:1; 61:1; 84:120; 95:7

BELOVED

GOD'S BELOVED SON

The phrase used most often by the Father in introducing and identi-fying Jesus is "my beloved Son" (Matthew 3:17). Jesus deserved to be *beloved* of the Father for many reasons, not the least of which were His firstborn primacy among the spirit children of the Father; the reality that He was the literal, physical son of the Father; and His unequaled righteousness in obeying the Father.

MATTHEW 3:17; 12:18; 17:5; 2 NEPHI 31:11, 15;
3 NEPHI 11:7; 21:20; DOCTRINE AND COVENANTS 93:15;
MOSES 4:2; JOSEPH SMITH—HISTORY 1:17

BISHOP AND SHEPHERD OF YOUR SOULS

This title of *Bishop* comes from a Greek word meaning "overseer." A bishop is literally *a watcher*. Combined with the title *Shepherd*, this title suggests Jesus's earnest oversight of His flock, all of whom need care and protection.

1 PETER 2:25

BRANCH

BRANCH OF THE LORD
BRANCH OF RIGHTEOUSNESS

The imagery here is a favorite in ancient Israel: the tree or vine with its roots, branches, and fruit. In one application Christ is the "righteous Branch" coming out of the root of David (Jeremiah 23:5), by whom He will claim His mortal kingship. On other occasions He is the "stem" undergirding life (Isaiah 11:1) or the "vine" out of whom we are to be branches (John 15:1–5) in producing fruitful lives.

ISAIAH 4:2; 11:1–5; JEREMIAH 33:15; ZECHARIAH 3:8; 6:12

Bread

BREAD OF GOD

BREAD OF LIFE

—— ✦ ——

In one of the most defining (and to some, most offensive) sermons He ever gave, Jesus said to those who sought temporal food that what He offered was another kind of nourishment: bread sent from God, true bread, living bread, bread sent from heaven. Then He shocked all by saying He was that bread. He declared that whosoever would eat of the bread that He gave—meaning His own bodily sacrifice—would have eternal life. In making this statement He alluded to the ordinance of the sacrament, which He would later institute just before beginning His atoning sacrifice. In this instance, many who had come to listen to Him left His presence, rejecting His offer of bread (Himself). Even today in the Middle East, it is considered to be discourteous, a violation of the sacred law of hospitality, to decline an offer of bread or set it aside as unfit to use. That is precisely what this congregation did with Jesus's offer of salvation.

JOHN 6:32, 33, 35, 41, 48, 50, 51, 58

BRIDEGROOM

—— ✦ ——

A common metaphor for ancient Israel's relationship to Jehovah was as bride to bridegroom in a marriage covenant. Later that same analogy was made in New Testament times, highlighting the relationship of the members of the church to Jesus Christ. Spiritual adultery was declared in those instances in which Israel or the church (the bride) was not faithful to the Bridegroom. The Second Coming of the Lord is likened to the Bridegroom coming to claim His bride, a moment for which all should be prepared, worthy, and dressed properly for the celebration.

MATTHEW 9:15; 22:1–12; 25:1–13; JOHN 3:29;
DOCTRINE AND COVENANTS 33:17–18; 65:3; 88:92; 133:10

BRIGHT AND MORNING STAR

—— ✦ ——

See Dayspring; Day Star; Star

REVELATION 2:28; 22:16

BUCKLER

———— ➤·◄ ————

Buckler is an archaic synonym for *shield*. A buckler was often round in shape, with straps on the back through which the warrior would insert one arm while wielding a sword or similar weapon with the other. The meaning rests in Christ's protection for those who have faith in Him.

2 SAMUEL 22:31; PSALMS 18:2; 91:4; PROVERBS 2:7;
DOCTRINE AND COVENANTS 35:14

CAPTAIN OF SALVATION

———— ➤·◄ ————

The "captain of [our] salvation" is a name given to the Lord in the Epistle to the Hebrews. The title is self-explanatory, noting that Christ is the source of and instrument in our salvation, the leader of those whom He is guiding and directing to exaltation. "The captain of the Lord's host" is the name given to the angel, interpreted by some to be Jehovah, who appeared to several Old Testament prophets (see, for example, Genesis 2:1, 7; Exodus 3:2, 6). In the King James Version, there are no fewer than thirteen Hebrew words and four different Greek words that are translated as *captain* in the English text.

JOSHUA 5:14–15; HEBREWS 2:10

CARPENTER

SON OF THE CARPENTER

—— ➤•◄ ——

It was the tradition for every Jew, including the rabbis, to learn a trade or a practical skill. This is an obvious reference to the work of Jesus's foster father, Joseph, and the training young Jesus presumably received at his hand.

It is interesting that this is the only title for Jesus (except perhaps *Shepherd*, which has a dual meaning) that applies to His temporal life as opposed to the myriad others that highlight His divine attributes and underscore His spiritual calling.

MATTHEW 13:55; MARK 6:3

CHIEF CORNER STONE

———— ➤•◄ ————

See Stone

EPHESIANS 2:20; 1 PETER 2:6–8

Chosen

CHOSEN OF GOD

CHOSEN FROM THE BEGINNING

———— ➤•◄ ————

This is a reference to the Father's choice of the premortal Jesus for the duty *someone* had to assume to atone for the sins of humankind in mortality.

LUKE 23:35; 1 PETER 2:4; MOSES 4:2; 7:39

CHRIST

———— ✦·◄ ————

See also Anointed One; Messiah

*T*his is one of the two most frequently used titles for Jesus in all of scripture, appearing more than 1,100 times in the standard works, with only the given name *Jesus* appearing more often (the latter just under 1,300 times.) The title *Christ*—arguably the most esteemed of religious titles because it meant *deliverance* to the people, both politically and spiritually—comes from the Greek word *cristos,* which means "to anoint," or the "anointed one," the same meaning that the Hebrew word *Messiah* carries. The word is frequently linked with the name *Jesus,* with or without the article *the* connecting them. At least three times the Savior accepted this description of Himself (see Matthew 16:16–17; Mark 14:61–62; John 4:25–26).

In the Israelite tradition, to anoint someone was to pour out on the head the oil of the holy priesthood and confirm it with a spoken blessing as prompted by the Holy Spirit. This was done in several circumstances, but it was most celebrated in the divine commission that God, through His ordained leaders, gave to kings for their political reign and to prophets for their spiritual ministry. The premortal Jesus was anointed and prepared for both roles, kingly and prophetic, though they were seldom recognized during His mortal ministry.

Following are examples of titles or roles that are sometimes associated with the title *Christ*, giving further insight into His anointed, messianic mission.

Christ a Righteous Judge

MOSES 6:57

Christ, Great God and Our Saviour Jesus

TITUS 2:13

Christ, His

REVELATION 11:15; 12:10

Christ Jesus

ACTS 19:4; 1 TIMOTHY 2:5; ALMA 5:44

Christ, Jesus

ROMANS 6:3; 2 NEPHI 25:19;

DOCTRINE AND COVENANTS 35:2

Christ Jesus Our Lord

ROMANS 8:39

Christ, Jesus the

MATTHEW 16:20

Christ Jesus the Lord

COLOSSIANS 2:6

Christ, Lord and

ACTS 2:36

Christ, Lord and Savior Jesus

DOCTRINE AND COVENANTS 20:1, 30

Christ, My God and My Savior Jesus
3 NEPHI 5:20

Christ of God
LUKE 9:20

Christ of Nazareth
ACTS 3:6

Christ Our Lord
ROMANS 5:1

Christ, Our Lord and Savior Jesus
2 PETER 1:11; DOCTRINE AND COVENANTS 20:1, 30

Christ, Our Lord Jesus
PHILIPPIANS 4:23

Christ Our Lord, Son Jesus
ROMANS 1:3

Christ Our Passover
1 CORINTHIANS 5:7

Christ Our Saviour
TITUS 1:4; 3:6

Christ the Firstfruits
1 CORINTHIANS 15:23

Christ the King of Israel
MARK 15:32

Christ the Lamb
DOCTRINE AND COVENANTS 76:85

Christ the Lord

LUKE 2:11; DOCTRINE AND COVENANTS 19:1

Christ the Lord God Omnipotent

MOSIAH 5:15

Christ, the Lord Jesus

1 CORINTHIANS 8:6; PHILIPPIANS 3:20;

MOSIAH 3:12

Christ the Lord Omnipotent

MOSIAH 3:17

Christ, the Lord's

LUKE 2:26

Christ the Righteous

1 JOHN 2:1

Christ the Same Yesterday, and To Day, and For Ever

HEBREWS 13:8

Christ the Son

ALMA 11:44

Christ the Son of God

MATTHEW 26:63; 3 NEPHI 9:15;

DOCTRINE AND COVENANTS 35:2

Christ Your Lord and Your Redeemer

DOCTRINE AND COVENANTS 15:1

Christ Your Redeemer

DOCTRINE AND COVENANTS 34:1

CONFIDENCE

The psalmist speaks of Jehovah being "the confidence of all the ends of the earth, and of them that are afar off upon the sea" (Psalm 65:5). *Confidence* is used routinely as a noun elsewhere in scripture, but nowhere else is it personified as it is here. The Hebrew word that translates as *confidence* originally meant "to be open," suggesting that where nothing is hidden, a person can feel safe and confident. The same word is sometimes translated as *trust* or *assurance*. Deity is the *source* of our confidence, as well as the unfailing *object* of our trust.

JOB 31:24

CONSOLATION OF ISRAEL

Consolation has at least two meanings. The most common is the solace (note the Latin root *sola* in both words, meaning "to comfort") given to one who is disappointed or defeated. The less common meaning applies to one who offers that solace and comfort. It is this latter personification of the word that applies to Jesus, who would bring joy to counter Israel's disappointment and victory to overcome her defeat. The Greek word translated as *consolation* here is similar to the word translated as *comforter* in the Gospel of John.

LUKE 2:25; JOHN 14:16

CORNERSTONE

———— ➤·◄ ————

See Stone

PSALM 118:22; ISAIAH 28:16; EPHESIANS 2:20; 1 PETER 2:6–8

COUNSELOR

———— ➤·◄ ————

The person to whom one wants to go if counsel is needed is one who is attentive, sympathetic, and wise. Many skilled mortals can offer these qualities to the seeker. How wonderful it would be if that Counselor were also omniscient, omnipotent, and omnipresent. The Father and the Son offer the former virtues shared with mortals and the latter characteristics possessed only by Deity. They are the perfect Counselors.

ISAIAH 9:6; 2 NEPHI 19:6

COVENANT OF
THE PEOPLE

———— ➤•◄ ————

God has made covenants with His children since the time He introduced the idea of covenant to Adam and Eve. Indeed, one of the essential purposes of mortal life in a fallen world is to participate in saving ordinances through which we make covenants with God and each other. Christ is the grand central figure in making those covenants and ordinances efficacious in time and eternity. He is the sacrifice upon which the covenant is based, whose blood ratifies it, and He is also the Mediator of the Covenant.

It should be noted that *covenant* is also a synonym for *testament*. An example of that usage is when the Lord told the early Latter-day Saints to "remember the new covenant, even the Book of Mormon" (Doctrine and Covenants 84:57). That sentence could just as easily have read "remember the new [or another] testament, even the Book of Mormon."

JEREMIAH 31:31–34; MATTHEW 26:28; 1 CORINTHIANS 11:25;
HEBREWS 12:24; 1 NEPHI 21:8; MOSES 5:4–9

Creator

EXCEPT FOR THE CREATION OF THE SPIRITS AND
BODIES OF INDIVIDUAL MEN AND WOMEN, A ROLE
RESERVED FOR GOD THE FATHER, ALL OTHER
ELEMENTS OF CREATION REGARDING EARTH LIFE
WERE ACCOMPLISHED BY JESUS CHRIST UNDER
THE DIRECTION OF THE FATHER.

ISAIAH 40:28; JOHN 1:1–3; 2 NEPHI 9:5;
DOCTRINE AND COVENANTS 38:1–4; 76:24; 93:6–10;
MOSES 1:32–33

Below are examples of titles or roles that are sometimes associated with the title *Creator*, giving further insight into His premortal majesty.

Creator, Faithful

1 PETER 4:19

Creator, Great

2 NEPHI 9:5–6

Creator of All Things from the Beginning

HELAMAN 14:12

Creator of Heaven and Earth, All Powerful

JACOB 2:5; DOCTRINE AND COVENANTS 14:9

Creator of Israel

ISAIAH 43:15

Creator of the Ends of the Earth

ISAIAH 40:28

Creator of the First Day

DOCTRINE AND COVENANTS 95:7

Creator of the Heavens

ISAIAH 42:5

Creator of the Wind

AMOS 4:13

Creator, Supreme

ALMA 30:44

CROWN OF GLORY
DIADEM OF BEAUTY

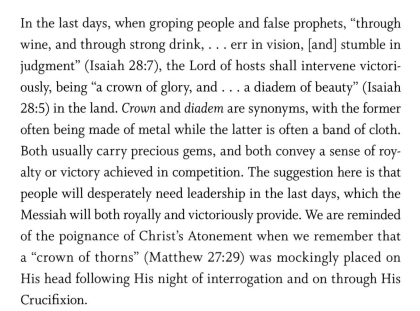

In the last days, when groping people and false prophets, "through wine, and through strong drink, . . . err in vision, [and] stumble in judgment" (Isaiah 28:7), the Lord of hosts shall intervene victoriously, being "a crown of glory, and . . . a diadem of beauty" (Isaiah 28:5) in the land. *Crown* and *diadem* are synonyms, with the former often being made of metal while the latter is often a band of cloth. Both usually carry precious gems, and both convey a sense of royalty or victory achieved in competition. The suggestion here is that people will desperately need leadership in the last days, which the Messiah will both royally and victoriously provide. We are reminded of the poignance of Christ's Atonement when we remember that a "crown of thorns" (Matthew 27:29) was mockingly placed on His head following His night of interrogation and on through His Crucifixion.

ISAIAH 28:5–9; MATTHEW 27:29; HEBREWS 2:9

DAVID

ROOT OF DAVID
SEED OF DAVID
SON OF DAVID
OFFSPRING OF DAVID

———— ➤•◄ ————

The Old Testament prophets provide the most useful ties between King David of old and King David (Christ) in the last days. Jeremiah wrote:

"Behold, the days come, saith the Lord, that I will raise unto David a righteous Branch, and a King shall reign and prosper, and shall execute judgment and justice in the earth.

"In his days Judah shall be saved, and Israel shall dwell safely: and this is his name whereby he shall be called, The Lord Our Righteousness" (Jeremiah 23:5–6).

Shortly thereafter Ezekiel prophesied:

"David my servant shall be king over them: and they all shall have one shepherd: they shall also walk in my judgments, and observe my statutes, and do them.

"And they shall dwell in the land that I have given unto Jacob my servant, wherein your fathers have dwelt: and they shall dwell therein, even they, and their children, and their children's children for ever: and my servant David shall be their prince for ever" (Ezekiel 37:24–25).

In his marvelous apocalyptic revelation, John made very explicit reference to the root of David:

"And I wept much, because no man was found worthy to open and to read the book, neither to look thereon.

"And one of the elders saith unto me, Weep not: behold, the Lion of the tribe of Juda, the Root of David, hath prevailed to open the book, and to loose the seven seals thereof. . . .

"I Jesus have sent mine angel to testify unto you these things in the churches. I am the root and the offspring of David, *and* the bright and morning star" (Revelation 5:4–5; 22:16).

It should be noted that *root* in this context means "He who descended from David," not "he from whom David descended." The name means "dear, well-beloved."

ISAIAH 11:1, 10; MATTHEW 1:1; 9:27;

LUKE 20:41; ROMANS 15:12; 2 TIMOTHY 2:8

DAYSPRING

———— ✦·◄ ————

This is the title used for Jesus by Zacharias, father of John who would become the Baptist. After prophesying of John's mission to prepare the way of the Savior, this great high priest noted the light Jesus would bring "to them that sit in darkness and in the shadow of death" (Luke 1:79). *Dayspring* is yet another metaphor for the dawning of the morning light after the darkness of night so many experience. It is a synonym for the Son/Sun that will always rise on those who patiently wait for and trust in it.

LUKE 1:76–78; ISAIAH 60:1–2

DAY STAR

———— ✦·◄ ————

As with *dayspring, day star* comes from Peter's injunction to members of the Church to trust in and wait for the light that will come with the appearance of the Son/Sun in the last days, or other experiences when "the more sure word of prophecy" is manifest (Doctrine and Covenants 131:5). Peter also suggests that we can lean on the faith of others during those dark nights of our lives "until the day dawn, and the day star arise in your hearts," at which time we will have our own witness and personal testimony (2 Peter 1:19).

DELIVERER

MY HELP AND DELIVERER

DELIVERER FROM DEATH AND THE CHAINS OF HELL

———— ➤•◄ ————

Christ delivers us from a variety of difficulties and dangers, ranging from childish predicaments to the starkness of death and hell. We are delivered from Adam's transgression unconditionally but delivered from our own transgressions conditioned upon our repentance. Another less obvious but provocative definition of *deliver* is to "bring forth," as in *delivering* a child at birth. Certainly, Christ is also our Deliverer in that sense, giving us new life and rebirth as we become His sons and daughters spiritually.

PSALM 40:17; ROMANS 4:25; 11:26; MOSIAH 5:7–8;

DOCTRINE AND COVENANTS 8:2–4; 133:67, 71–72

DESIRE OF ALL NATIONS

———— ➤·◄ ————

In the last days good people across the world will yearn for the return of Jesus to rule in righteousness and introduce millennial peace. After God "shake[s] all nations" (Haggai 2:7), His answer to the prayers of the people—Christ, the Desire of All Nations—shall come. In that usage *Desire* is a noun, a proper name. The act of desiring on the part of the people is a verb, akin to "hunger[ing] and thirst[ing] after righteousness" (Matthew 5:6).

DOOR OF THE SHEEP

———— ➤·◄ ————

See Sheep; Shepherd

JOHN 10:7, 9

DREADFUL

———— ➤·◄ ————

Although the titles Christ carries are usually soothing and encouraging, from time to time He reminds us there is a part of Him that is wholeheartedly opposed to disobedience and sin. That is *not* soothing. "My name is dreadful" (Malachi 1:14), He warns those who do not follow Him, "the great and dreadful God" (Daniel 9:4).

ELECT

ELECT OF GOD

This word comes from a Latin root meaning "chosen" or "selected." *Elite* has the same root, suggesting a particularly lofty achievement. In contemporary times, *election* often refers to being chosen for an office or position of authority. Christ qualifies on all these counts; He is known as the "Elect" among God's spiritual offspring in both the Old and New Testaments.

ISAIAH 42:1; 1 PETER 2:6

EMMANUEL

IMMANUEL

A title given to Jesus at His birth meaning "God with us" (Matthew 1:23). Matthew obviously felt that Christ's Nativity fulfilled the prophecy of Isaiah (made some seven centuries before) that the baby should be identified as such. Joseph Smith used this title for Christ when he gave a rousing call to members of the Church of Jesus Christ to participate in the work of redemption.

ISAIAH 7:14; MATTHEW 1:23; 2 NEPHI 18:8;

DOCTRINE AND COVENANTS 128:22

END

See Alpha and Omega; Beginning and End

ROMANS 10:4; REVELATION 1:8;
DOCTRINE AND COVENANTS 35:1; 38:1

The significance of this title is that the word is traditionally used in scripture as an adjective modifying a noun, whereas in modern revelation the word is appropriately used as a noun itself. Thus, in traditional usage a phrase like "endless punishment" (with *endless* as an adjective) would have meant punishment that never ended. However, with *endless* as a noun—a name for Deity—*endless* punishment means it is God's punishment, thus taking on a qualitative rather than quantitative meaning.

DOCTRINE AND COVENANTS 19:10–12

Eternal

As in the example cited previously for *endless*, the word eternal is used the same way in the same scriptural reference (Doctrine and Covenants 19:11). Furthermore, such a title appropriately refers to "him which is, and which was, and which is to come" (Revelation 1:4), "which art, and wast, and shalt be" (Revelation 16:5), "which is, and which was, and which is to come, the Almighty" (Revelation 1:8), "infinite and eternal" (Doctrine and Covenants 20:17), "who is from all eternity to all eternity" (Doctrine and Covenants 39:1).

JST, REVELATION 1:4, 8; ALMA 34:10, 14

Other linked descriptions include:

Eternal Father of Heaven and of Earth

ALMA 11:39

Eternal Father, the Very

MOSIAH 15:4; 16:15

Eternal God

1 NEPHI 12:18

Eternal Head

HELAMAN 13:38

Eternal Judge

MORONI 10:34

Eternal King

DOCTRINE AND COVENANTS 128:23

Eternal Life

1 JOHN 1:2; 5:20

EVERLASTING

See also Alpha and Omega;
Beginning and End; Eternal

The obvious meaning here is the eternal, never-ending reality of Christ's divinity. Its most well-known use comes in Isaiah's majestic prophecy of the Messiah's birth, "And his name shall be called Wonderful, Counsellor, The mighty God, The Everlasting Father, The Prince of Peace" (Isaiah 9:6).

Other references include:

Everlasting Father

ISAIAH 9:6; 2 NEPHI 19:6

Everlasting God

ISAIAH 40:28; 1 NEPHI 15:15

Everlasting God, My Rock and Mine

2 NEPHI 4:35

Everlasting King

JEREMIAH 10:10

Everlasting Light

ISAIAH 60:20

Everlasting Strength

ISAIAH 26:4

Everlasting to Everlasting

DOCTRINE AND COVENANTS 61:1

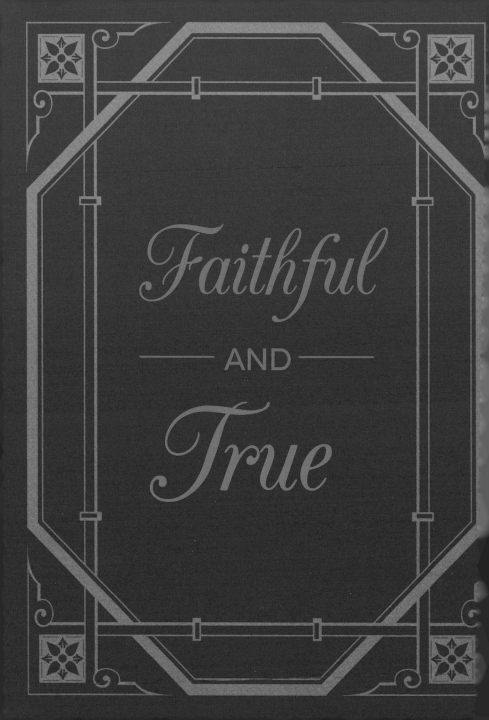

Faithful

— AND —

True

This title has at least two meanings, both of which are applicable to Him as the premortal Jehovah in the Old Testament and the mortal Jesus in His New Testament role. One meaning is that His faith never falters. If faith were a line drawn forward in the sand marking the course of the Savior's journey, there would be no break in that line. His faith is constant, always evident. He never strays from it, is always *true* to it. The other meaning is that He is full of faith—literally faithful. This interpretation suggests that everything about Him is characterized by faith, that it is His "first principle" just as it is supposed to be ours (Articles of Faith 1:4).

REVELATION 19:11

Other dimensions of this title include:

Faithful Creator

1 PETER 4:19

Faithful God

DEUTERONOMY 7:9

Faithful, Lord That Is

ISAIAH 49:7

Faithful Witness

REVELATION 1:5; 3:14

FATHER

————— ➤•◄ —————

Referring to Christ as "the Father" can cause some confusion in a theology that does not follow the trinitarian creeds of the fourth and fifth centuries AD. For that reason, it is important to make clear at the outset that Christ is not the Father of our spirits. That role and title belong to Elohim, who gave us spiritual existence and form. It is Elohim to whom Jesus prayed, and to whom He taught us to pray as "our Father which art in heaven" (Matthew 6:9).

Having said that, there are several ways in which Jesus is also a Father to us, the most important of which is that through His Atonement and Resurrection He gave us eternal life. He did this by breaking the bands of death for all humankind who would ever live, from Adam and Eve to the end of the world. Christ can also rightfully speak for God the Father through the "divine investiture of authority" given Him by the Father. Lastly, even before the Resurrection we can become the "sons and daughters" of Christ by making sacred covenants with Him and keeping His commandments in honor of those covenants. In that way we are "spiritually begotten" of Him and "born of him" (Mosiah 5:7).

We are so used to saying and hearing the word *Father* that we may forget—or never really have known—that the Latin root means "nourisher," "protector," "upholder," and "one who holds a position of counsel and care." Those are reassuring qualities for any Father to have, qualities Christ had in abundance.

Other citations and qualifications of the title include:

Father and the Son

MOSIAH 15:2–3; ETHER 3:14

Father, Everlasting

ISAIAH 9:6; 2 NEPHI 19:6

Father, Lord God of Israel our

1 CHRONICLES 29:10

Father of All Things

MOSIAH 7:27

Father of Heaven and of Earth

MOSIAH 3:8; HELAMAN 14:12

Father of Heaven and of Earth, the Very Eternal

MOSIAH 15:4; ALMA 11:39

Father of the Fatherless

PSALM 68:5

Father, Our

ISAIAH 64:8

Father That Hath Bought Thee

DEUTERONOMY 32:6

Father, the Very Eternal

MOSIAH 16:15

Father to Israel

JEREMIAH 31:9

FINISHER OF
OUR FAITH

———— ➤·◄ ————

He who was the Author of salvation in its beginning is also the Finisher of it in the end. Carrying that title, Christ will complete our piecemeal and uneven faith. *Finish* also has a qualitative meaning that is appropriate here: that of bringing the product to its highest level of appearance and presentation, as in the fine "finish" one would give to a piece of art or craftmanship.

HEBREWS 12:2; MORONI 6:4

FIRE

WALL OF FIRE

CONSUMING FIRE

Jehovah's presence and glory are often portrayed in the language of flame and fire. When the children of Israel needed guidance on their quest for the Promised Land, Jehovah went before them "by day time in a pillar of a cloud, and in a pillar of fire by night" (Numbers 14:14). When He needed to instruct Moses directly, He descended on Mount Sinai "in fire" (Exodus 19:18). To the prophet Zechariah, who prophesied so much of the mortal mission of Jesus Christ and His triumphant Second Coming, He said of Jerusalem in the last days, "For I, saith the Lord, will be unto her a wall of fire round about, and will be the glory in the midst of her" (Zechariah 2:5). Truly God is a "consuming fire" (Hebrews 12:29).

On the altar of the wilderness tabernacle ancient Israel's prophets kept a fire constantly burning. One of its purposes was to consume the burnt sacrifice and incense offering, but another was to remind the children of Israel that Jehovah was always with them. Fire was frequently the symbol of God's spiritual presence among the people, reminding them among other things of His glory (Daniel 7:9; 10:6), His holiness (Exodus 19:18), and His protection (Zechariah 2:5). For those who needed it, it was also a reminder of His judgments (Isaiah 66:15–16) and punishment (Matthew 25:41).

EXODUS 13:21–22; DEUTERONOMY 4:24; NEHEMIAH 9:12;
REVELATION 1:14; DOCTRINE AND COVENANTS 110:3

FIRST AND LAST

—— ➤•◄ ——

See also Alpha and Omega; Beginning and End; Eternal; Everlasting

Once again we see the all-encompassing dimensions of Christ's ministry. He was the first in the premortal world of God's spirit offspring. He was the first in worthiness to become the mortal Son of God. He was the firstfruit of the Resurrection, and He will be the last—not only in chronological order but also in ultimate significance—in His triumphant return to rule and reign on earth.

ISAIAH 41:4; 44:6; REVELATION 1:11, 17; 2:8; 22:13; 1 NEPHI 20:12; ALMA 11:39; DOCTRINE AND COVENANTS 110:4

Related titles include:

Firstbegotten
HEBREWS 1:6

Firstbegotten of the Dead
REVELATION 1:5

Firstborn
PSALM 89:27; LUKE 2:7; ROMANS 8:29; COLOSSIANS 1:15, 18; DOCTRINE AND COVENANTS 93:21

Firstfruit(s)
1 CORINTHIANS 15:20, 23

Forerunner

U sually we think of Elias, John the Baptist, or some other pioneering figure as the one who goes before, preparing the way for others to follow. There is, however, at least one sense in which Christ was also a forerunner. In that role He went before us preparing the way of salvation and conquering death, experiencing all the pain of our sins and sorrows, our illnesses and our limitations, in order that He could succor us when we too walk that same path. In all things He was a *forerunner* in preparing us to reenter the presence of the Father (see John 14:1–6).

HEBREWS 6:20; ALMA 7:11–12;

DOCTRINE AND COVENANTS 122:8

FOUNDATION

———— ➤·◄ ————

Using the familiar Church-as-a-building metaphor, Paul declared Jesus as the *foundation* of the righteous building this Apostle and His brethren were attempting to build through missionary work.

> "For we are labourers together with God: ye are God's husbandry, ye are God's building.
>
> "According to the grace of God which is given unto me, as a wise masterbuilder, I have laid the foundation, and another buildeth thereon. But let every man take heed how he buildeth thereupon.
>
> "For other foundation can no man lay than that is laid, which is Jesus Christ" (1 Corinthians 3:9–11; emphasis added).

This is consistent with other references to Christ as, for example, the cornerstone of the Church.

FOUNTAIN

FOUNTAIN OF LIVING WATERS

FOUNTAIN OF ALL RIGHTEOUSNESS

FOUNTAIN OF LIFE

———— ✦•◀ ————

Christ is the source of eternal life, the headwaters of all righteousness, the example to whom we look for a perfect life. It is from Him we learn, by Him we live, and for Him we serve—all in the name of the Father. From Christ is that fountain from which, if we drink, will be "water springing up into everlasting life" (John 4:14).

PSALM 36:9; JEREMIAH 2:13;
JOHN 4:10–14; 1 NEPHI 11:25

FRAMER OF HEAVEN AND EARTH

———— ➤·◄ ————

See also Creator

Framer could justifiably be considered simply a synonym for *Creator,* as it is in a phrase like "framers of the Constitution." This is a perfectly satisfactory explanation of this title. However, a *framer* in an earlier era of construction was always a carpenter, a craftsman who fashioned the exterior and interior walls, rooms, and hallways of a home or shop by the upright timbers he put in place that gave the structure its shape and dimensions. Perhaps there is special meaning in the fact that the carpenter's son from Nazareth was a *framer* long before He came to earth to learn building skills in His foster father's shop. A *framer* can also be one who brings definition and completeness to a project, as one who *frames* a piece of art—another apt description of the Savior's work.

EPHESIANS 2:21; 4:16; DOCTRINE AND COVENANTS 20:17

GIFT OF GOD
HIS UNSPEAKABLE GIFT

Perhaps the only gift in all of creation that matches the gift of immortality and eternal life provided by the Savior through His Atonement is the gift that God the Father made in allowing His Only Begotten Son to come to earth and redeem all mankind through the pain of that Atonement. "For God so loved the world" (John 3:16) may be one of the most understated and underappreciated truths in all of scripture.

JOHN 4:10; 2 CORINTHIANS 9:15

Glory

GLORIOUS

——— ➤◄ ———

When Moses was confronted by Lucifer pretending to be the chosen son of God, this great prophet could discern the misrepresentation. By comparison, Lucifer did not possess the true Spirit or convey the full presence of divine glory. Moses rebuked Satan by declaring his loyalty to Jehovah, the God of Glory. In several places in the scriptures, the glory of Deity is described as majesty, brightness, and splendor.

ISAIAH 4:5; ZECHARIAH 2:5; ACTS 22:11;

HEBREWS 1:3; MOSES 1:20

Other references to this divine quality include:

Glorious Majesty on High
DOCTRINE AND COVENANTS 20:16

Glorious Throne to His Father's House
ISAIAH 22:23

Glory, Lord of
1 CORINTHIANS 2:8

Glory of Their Strength
PSALM 89:17

Glory of Thy People
LUKE 2:32

Glory of Zion
2 NEPHI 14:5

God

This is the title commonly given by believers (and frequently by nonbelievers) to Him who is the Supreme Being, the Man of Holiness, the Father of Spirits, and the literal Father of Jesus Christ. According to one electronic search procedure, there are a total of 7,681 references to *God* in our Latter-day Saint edition of the scriptures. However, not all of these refer to God the Father. Jesus also is a God by virtue of His role in the Creation, His role as Jehovah of the Old Testament, His divine sonship as the literal offspring of the Father, His perfect mortal life, and His ascension after His Resurrection to stand on the right hand of God the Father. There, with the Holy Ghost, these three form the grand Triumvirate, a unified Godhead who are One in virtually every sense of that word *except* in corporeal substance.

In many cases the scriptures are not clear whether *God* applies to the Father or to Jesus in His own godly role. However, it is not necessary in this study to declare which reference goes with what Personage; here we are dealing only with titles, and many of the titles are interchangeable between the Father and the Son, applying equally to both. *God* and *Lord* are two such titles wherein it is often impossible to determine whether they apply to the Father or the Son.

With no attempt to exhaust all references
and distinctive identifications, the following
are noted as representative:

God Himself That Formed the Earth and Made It
ISAIAH 45:18

God, Jesus as
ISAIAH 9:6; 40:3, 9, 10; JOHN 20:28

God My Rock, My Saviour
2 SAMUEL 22:3

*God of Compassion, Gracious[ness],
Longsuffering, Mercy, and Truth*
PSALM 86:15

God of Enoch
DOCTRINE AND COVENANTS 45:11

God of Glory
MOSES 1:20

God of Israel, the Saviour
ISAIAH 45:15; 1 NEPHI 19:7

God of Nature
1 NEPHI 19:12

God of Peace
ROMANS 16:20

God of Salvation

PSALM 18:46; ISAIAH 17:10;
1 CORINTHIANS 10:4; JACOB 7:25

God of the Land

ETHER 2:12

God of the Whole Earth

ISAIAH 54:5; 3 NEPHI 11:14; 22:5

God of Thy Fathers, of Your Fathers

ACTS 7:32; EXODUS 3:13

God of Truth without Iniquity

DEUTERONOMY 32:4

God Our Saviour

PSALM 106:21; ISAIAH 43:3; 1 TIMOTHY 1:1

*God Ready to Pardon, Gracious and Merciful,
Slow to Anger, of Great Kindness*

NEHEMIAH 9:17

God the Lord

JOHN 20:28; DOCTRINE AND COVENANTS 1:20

God, Uncorruptible

ROMANS 1:23

God with Us

MATTHEW 1:23

MIGHTY
GOD

The adjective in this title suggests power, which in Deity would be *all* power—omnipotence. Indeed, David sang that Jehovah was the "most mighty" of all, linking that power with other regal qualities such as "glory" and "majesty" (Psalm 45:3). As such He is the mighty One of Jacob (Israel) and is mighty to save.

GENESIS 49:24; ISAIAH 9:6; 60:16; 1 NEPHI 21:26; 22:12;
2 NEPHI 6:17; 19:6; DOCTRINE AND COVENANTS 36:1

MOST HIGH
GOD

Exaltation has always been couched in terms and images that suggest ascension, elevation, loftiness, heavenly attainment. Of those enjoying such spiritual elevation, Jesus, who stands at the right hand of the Father, holds the highest position among all of God's posterity.

PSALMS 57:2; 83:18; ACTS 7:48; 16:17; 2 NEPHI 24:14; ALMA 26:14

GOVERNOR

———— ➤•◄ ————

A *governor* is, quite obviously, one who governs. It was prophesied long before His birth that Christ would rule and reign, with "the government . . . upon his shoulder," and that such a governor would come out of tiny Bethlehem in Judea. The challenge of each individual in mortality is to allow Christ to govern as He was ordained to do, with all of us as good citizens obeying His commandments and receiving the blessings that come from a just ruler.

ISAIAH 9:6–7; MICAH 5:2; MATTHEW 2:6

GREAT I AM

———— ➤•◄ ————

See I Am

DOCTRINE AND COVENANTS 29:1; 38:1; 39:1

GREAT SHEPHERD OF THE SHEEP

Great is almost always an adjective rather than a title when it applies to the life and mission of the Savior. However, there are certain instances when it takes on the nature of a proper name, such as this reference in the Epistle to the Hebrews. This phrase conveys something of the spirit of a title, over and above what a simple reference to *shepherd* might convey (see Hebrews 13:20).

Other examples include:

Great, and Last, and Only Sure Foundation

JACOB 4:16

Great and True Shepherd

HELAMAN 15:13

Great Jehovah

MORONI 10:34; DOCTRINE AND COVENANTS 128:9

Great Mediator

2 NEPHI 2:27–28

Great Prophet

LUKE 7:16

HABITATION OF JUSTICE

————————— ➤◆◄ —————————

HIS UNIQUE PHRASE FROM JEREMIAH SUGGESTS NOT
ONLY THAT JEHOVAH IS JUST BUT ALSO THAT THE VERY
ENVIRONMENT IN WHICH HE REIGNS AND THE ATMOSPHERE
IN WHICH HE RULES IS CHARACTERIZED BY JUSTICE. HIS
PEOPLE CAN BE CONFIDENT, SAFE, AND FORTHCOMING IN
HIS PRESENCE, KNOWING THEIR JUDGMENT WILL BE JUST,
WHATEVER HIS RULING AS JUDGE MIGHT BE.

PSALMS 71:3; 89:14; 91:9; JEREMIAH 50:7

HEAD

HEAD OF EVERY MAN
HEAD OF THE CHURCH

Head conveys several qualities that apply directly to Jesus Christ. First of all, the head is the top, the apex, the ultimate figure in an organization or congregation. Christ is that figure in the Church under the Fatherhood of God. As such, we are to follow His direction and example. Second, the head is home to the mind, which, along with the heart, everyone is to give to God in the effort to build Zion. Lastly, the head is the source, the origin, the beginning, as indicated in a word like *headwaters*. Christ is the source of our salvation and exaltation, the originating point for all that flows from the gospel of Jesus Christ into eternity.

In establishing the line of priesthood accountability, Paul wrote, "I would have you know, that the head of every man is Christ; . . . and the head of Christ is God" (1 Corinthians 11:3). This reinforced the Savior's own declaration that "No man cometh unto the Father, but by me" (John 14:6). That role, which He plays in every individual relationship, is the one He fulfills in His relationship to the Church as a whole. Paul continued, "Christ is the head of the church: . . . Therefore . . . the church is subject unto Christ, . . . even as Christ . . . loved the church, and gave himself for it" (Ephesians 5:23–25).

EPHESIANS 4:14–15; COLOSSIANS 1:18; JACOB 4:17; HELAMAN 13:38

HEIR OF ALL THINGS

God the Father has promised that those who receive Him will receive His kingdom, "therefore all that my Father hath shall be given unto him" (Doctrine and Covenants 84:38). While that is a promise given to all, the only person (of whom we know) who has received the Father fully and completely, without compromise or transgression, is Jesus Christ. Therefore, what is conditional and still hoped for by everyone else has already been realized by His Firstborn Son, who rightfully claims His inheritance as "heir of all things" (Hebrews 1:2). He even portrays Himself as an heir in a very moving parable He taught regarding His rejection and Crucifixion by the people (see Matthew 21:33–39).

HELPER

A *helper* is a companion, a supporter, an assistant, an ally. Christ is certainly all of these to those who will accept His offer.

PSALMS 10:14; 27:9; 30:10; 37:40; 40:17; 46:1; 124:8; ISAIAH 41:10–14; 49:8; MATTHEW 15:25; MARK 9:22–24; HEBREWS 13:6; JACOB 2:5

Highest

This is another example of a title most frequently associated with God the Father. Nevertheless, Jesus also merited that same nomenclature.

LUKE 1:76

HIGH PRIEST

Both in ancient and modern times, the *high priest* is the priesthood officer authorized to preside over the spiritual functions of the kingdom, including the offering of sacrifices. Christ qualified doubly for this designation, being the ultimate source of spiritual direction for the Church and also serving personally as the infinite and eternal sacrifice. Out of deference to the sanctity of the Savior's name we currently refer to the high priesthood as the holy Melchizedek Priesthood, but its true title is the Holy Priesthood, after the Order of the Son of God (see Doctrine and Covenants 107:1–4). Ultimately the holy priesthood is Christ's priesthood and He is the Great High Priest in that Order.

HEBREWS 2:17; 3:1; 4:15; 5:5–6, 10; 6:20: 8:1; 10:21

HIGH PRIEST OF GOOD THINGS TO COME

—— ➤ ◆ ◄ ——

This is such a unique designation I have separated it from the many other references to Christ's high priestly role. He is the Great High Priest in so many ways, but for a multitude of people—indeed, for all of us at some time or other in life—He is the High Priest of Hope. Because of Him things will get better. Because of Him there are always "good things to come" (Hebrews 9:11). The Father and the Son, the Holy Ghost and the angels who attend Them—Their entire employment, Their entire work is to seek ways to bless us. They who never sleep, They who never slumber, seek day and night for ways to bless us. We have our agency so there are some limits to what They *can* do, but They are constantly at work to bless us with good things to come if we but live for them.

HIGH PRIEST OF OUR PROFESSION

———— ➤·◄ ————

Having already noted Christ's role as High Priest, the addition of the phrase of *our profession* makes two interpretations possible. Perhaps the most obvious inclination in the twenty-first century would be to define *profession* as one's vocation or business affiliation, such as the *medical profession*. But it is unlikely this is the meaning intended here. It is much more likely that *profession* refers back to its original meaning, which was an avowal, a declaration of one's belief or the acceptance of a particular faith, as in the *professing* of Christianity. The Latin root for this word—*professio*—meant the taking of vows to join a religious order, the kind of decidedly religious *profession* that must have been intended by the writer of the Epistle to the Hebrews, who uses the word three times.

HEBREWS 3:1; 4:14; 10:23

HIMSELF

————— ➤•◄ —————

Here Matthew is quoting Isaiah, using a pronoun as a noun-title. Perhaps the intention of an Old Testament prophet and a New Testament Apostle in making *Himself* a title is to remind us that Christ and Christ alone carried the weight of the Atonement on His shoulders, that He Himself with help from no other has "trodden the wine-press alone" (Doctrine and Covenants 76:107).

MATTHEW 8:17;
DOCTRINE AND COVENANTS 88:106; 133:50

Anything worthy of the designation *holy* would, by definition, be sacred, consecrated, otherworldly, and reverential. Perhaps more than any other word in the religious vocabulary, this term speaks to the spiritual essence of a person or place or item with virtually *no* consideration of external qualities or temporal characteristics. Truly Christ was holy, and "holy is his name" (Luke 1:49). That phrase can be read at least two ways—with *holy* as an adjective and as a noun-title.

ISAIAH 6:3; HEBREWS 7:26; 1 PETER 1:15–16;

REVELATION 6:10

This same dual reading applies in several other ways, including:

Holy Child, Jesus
ACTS 4:27; MORONI 8:3

Holy God
JOSHUA 24:19; 2 NEPHI 9:39

Holy Messiah
2 NEPHI 2:6

Holy One, and Just
PSALM 16:10; ISAIAH 43:15; HOSEA 11:9; HABAKKUK 1:12;

ACTS 2:27; 3:14; 13:35; 1 JOHN 2:20; 2 NEPHI 2:10;

DOCTRINE AND COVENANTS 78:16

Holy One of God
MARK 1:24

Holy One of Israel, Thy Redeemer
ISAIAH 41:14; 43:14; 54:5; 1 NEPHI 19:14; 2 NEPHI 9:12, 15, 18–19

Holy One of Jacob
2 NEPHI 27:34

Holy One of Zion
DOCTRINE AND COVENANTS 78:15

HOPE

GOD OF HOPE
HOPE OF ISRAEL

———— ➤•◄ ————

A favorite definition of *hope* is "a happy anticipation, a confident expectation." Truly by that standard Christ is Hope personified. Our ultimate hope is in Him and in His Resurrection. As noted earlier, we always have hope for the future because He is "the high priest of good things to come" (Hebrews 9:11).

PSALM 71:5; JEREMIAH 14:8; 17:13, 17; 50:7; ROMANS 15:13;
COLOSSIANS 1:27; 1 TIMOTHY 1:1

HORN OF DAVID

———— ➤•◄ ————

See David

PSALM 132:17

HORN OF SALVATION

In ancient times a horn was used to declare some important event or noteworthy moment. It was also a symbol of power. Nothing could be more important or noteworthy than the declaration that Jesus Christ is the promised Messiah.

1 SAMUEL 2:10; 2 SAMUEL 22:3; PSALMS 18:2; 132:17; LUKE 1:69

HUSBAND

Husband has at least two meanings as it applies to Jesus Christ. First, one who *husbands* is one who nurtures, cultivates, nourishes, and brings to fruition. Second, in the Old Testament tradition, Jehovah is the Bridegroom and Israel is the bride, with that same relationship continuing into the mortal ties of the New Testament and beyond. In that divine marriage the Bridegroom takes on and fulfills all the caring, protective responsibilities of a dutiful Husband.

JEREMIAH 31:32; REVELATION 21:2; 3 NEPHI 22:5

I AM

I AM THAT I AM

THE GREAT I AM

———— ➤•◄ ————

See also Alpha and Omega; Beginning and End; Eternal; Everlasting

When Moses was told by Jehovah to confront the pharaoh of Egypt, he was afraid of rejection and the danger of such a bold move.

"Moses said unto God, Behold, when I come unto the children of Israel, and shall say unto them, The God of your fathers hath sent me unto you; and they shall say to me, What is his name? what shall I say unto them?

"And God said unto Moses, I AM THAT I AM: and he said, Thus shalt thou say unto the children of Israel, I AM hath sent me unto you" (Exodus 3:13–14).

This unusual title conveys at least two things about the Messiah: First, Jehovah/Christ emphatically is the promised Lord and Deliverer of covenant Israel (the spirit of "I am He"). Second, coming in the first-person-singular voice, this title carries the impact of presence, permanence, constancy, even eternity. *I Am* combines *I Was* and *I Will Be*, the Alpha and Omega quality to which we have already referred.

ISAIAH 44:6; 45:18; JOHN 8:58;

DOCTRINE AND COVENANTS 29:1; 38:1; 39:1; MOSES 7:53

IMAGE OF GOD

———— ✦·◄ ————

This is yet another example of a word that can be either adjective or noun-title—or both. *Image of God* can suggest how Christ was like the Father, but it can also be accepted as a complete phrase—that in one of His many divine roles Christ *was* the *Image of God*.

2 CORINTHIANS 4:4; COLOSSIANS 1:15; HEBREWS 1:3

Immanuel

———— ✦·◄ ————

See Emmanuel

JAH

Ancient Israel was forbidden to spell out the full name of Jehovah in any of its Hebraic variations and forms, which included *Yahweh, Yahwe, Yahveh, Yahve, Jahveh, Jahve, Jahweh,* and *Jahwe.* Instead, they would use abbreviated tetragrams (words of four letters) or, in this case, a trigram of three letters.

PSALM 68:4

JEALOUS

Jehovah was, of necessity, a jealous God in the sense that He emphatically wanted the loyalty of His children and could not bear to see them worship false deities. It was the kind of understandable emotion vividly recognized in another of Christ's roles, that of a Bridegroom whose bride had been unfaithful.

EXODUS 34:14; JOSHUA 24:19

JEHOVAH
THE GREAT JEHOVAH
LORD JEHOVAH

Among the people of ancient Israel, this was a well-known title for the God of the Old Testament, whom we know to have been the premortal Jesus acting under the direction of God the Father. It has been assumed that the word comes from the Hebrew verb *to be*. In that sense, it is comparable to I Am, Alpha and Omega, the Beginning and the End, and so forth, all conveying a permanent state, an unchanging presence. As noted under the heading JAH, the Jews were not to write out the full name of Jehovah (in Hebrew usually Yahweh) but used various trigrams or tetragrams as substitutes.

EXODUS 6:3; PSALM 83:18; ISAIAH 12:2; 26:4; 2 NEPHI 22:2;

MORONI 10:34; DOCTRINE AND COVENANTS 110:3

Jesus

See also Christ

Jesus is the Greek rendition of a name common among the Jews anciently and one still common in some romance languages. Its equivalent in Hebrew is Joshua, which translates as Savior. Joseph and Mary were directed by an angel to name her new son Jesus, "for he shall save his people from their sins" (Matthew 1:21).

1 THESSALONIANS 1:10; HEBREWS 4:14; 2 NEPHI 31:10; 33:6; DOCTRINE AND COVENANTS 45:52; 76:69

The addition of the more sacred word *Christ* to the common name Jesus elevates *Jesus Christ* to the divine status it merits in describing the mortal Son of God. Christ is the Greek title synonymous with the Hebrew Messiah, both words reserved for a foreordained person who would come to deliver His people as "the Anointed One." At least some of those who would recognize this Deliverer as the Christ/Messiah/Anointed One would also recognize Him as the Son of God and One with the Father.

2 NEPHI 10:3; 25:16–19; DOCTRINE AND COVENANTS 35:2

Other references to this redeemer of the world include:

Jesus Christ, by Whom Are All Things, and We by Him

1 CORINTHIANS 8:6

Jesus Christ, Great God and Our Saviour

TITUS 2:13

Jesus [Christ] of Nazareth, King of the Jews

MATTHEW 26:71; JOHN 19:19; ACTS 3:6

Jesus Christ, Our Lord

ROMANS 5:1

Jesus Christ Our Saviour

TITUS 3:6

Jesus Christ the Righteous, a Righteous Judge

1 JOHN 2:1; MOSES 6:57

Jesus Christ the Same Yesterday, and Today, and Forever

HEBREWS 13:8

Jesus Christ the Son of God

3 NEPHI 9:15

Jesus Christ, Your Lord and Your Redeemer

DOCTRINE AND COVENANTS 15:1

Jesus of Galilee

MATTHEW 26:69

Jesus the Christ

MATTHEW 16:20

JUDGE

OUR RIGHTEOUS JUDGE
JUDGE OF THE QUICK AND THE DEAD

A judge is committed to justice and equity. A judge is also subject to feelings of mercy and forgiveness. How reassuring it is that, accepting such responsibility with and under the direction of His Father (see Doctrine and Covenants 76:68), Jesus Christ shall be "the Eternal Judge of both quick and dead"—*quick* meaning "alive" or "living" (Moroni 10:34). He who knows everything about both justice and mercy will be seated in "the judgment-seat of Christ" (3 Nephi 28:31) before which "every soul who belongs to the whole human family of Adam" and Eve must stand to be judged of our works (Mormon 3:20).

JUDGES 11:27; PSALM 68:5; ISAIAH 33:22; MICAH 5:1; ACTS 10:42;

1 CORINTHIANS 4:4; 2 TIMOTHY 4:1, 8; 1 PETER 2:23; MOSIAH 3:18;

MORMON 6:21; ETHER 12:38; MORONI 8:21; MOSES 6:57

JUST

Here a virtue and a moral characteristic also serves as a title. He who was and is just takes on that virtue as part of His identity. Such usage indicates the perfect harmony between Jesus's nature and His actions. Knowing He is just allows one to come before Him with confidence and acceptance, knowing this judge will be fair and honest.

DEUTERONOMY 32:4; ISAIAH 45:21; ACTS 3:14; 7:52; ALMA 12:15

KEEPER OF THE GATE

It is an old religious fable that St. Peter will meet us at the gate of heaven. He (along with other key holders and witnesses of the gospel) may well be included there, but the principal gatekeeper will be the Lord Jesus Christ Himself, who "employeth no servant there" (2 Nephi 9:41).

King

This title refers to Christ's presiding role as "King of kings" (1 Timothy 6:15) in the theocratic governance of the kingdom of God both in heaven and on earth. Although it was without the intent to reign, Christ came as King in the meridian of time. But because he came "lowly, and riding upon . . . the foal of an ass" (Zechariah 9:9; see Matthew 21:1–7), His royalty was not recognized by any beyond a relative few who had eyes to see and ears to hear. To them and others on both sides of the veil who have taken upon themselves His name, Christ is still King, but to the rest of the human family He is King-in-Waiting until the time of His triumphant Second Coming. Then, as is appropriate in the presence of royalty, every knee shall bow and every tongue confess that He is the Messiah; the King of Zion; the True, Living, and Everlasting King of Nations; King over All the Earth.

ISAIAH 6:5; JEREMIAH 10:7, 10; ZECHARIAH 14:4–9; MALACHI 1:14; MATTHEW 27:42; 1 TIMOTHY 6:15–16; REVELATION 17:14; 19:16; DOCTRINE AND COVENANTS 38:21; 128:23; MOSES 7:53

Other references to Christ's royalty include:

King, Eternal

DOCTRINE AND COVENANTS 128:23

King Immanuel

DOCTRINE AND COVENANTS 128:22

King of Heaven

2 NEPHI 10:14

King of Israel

ZEPHANIAH 3:15; JOHN 1:49; 12:13

King of Peace

HEBREWS 7:2

King of Righteousness

HEBREWS 7:2

King of Saints

REVELATION 15:3

King of the Jews

MATTHEW 2:2; JOHN 19:19

King, the Lord of Hosts

2 NEPHI 16:5

LAMB

LAMB OF GOD

———— ➤·◄ ————

This is one of the titles—and responsibilities—that Christ received in the premortal councils of heaven. There the Father introduced the great plan of salvation that included, for those who accepted it, the fall and redemption of His children—the entire human family—in their journey toward exaltation. Adam and Eve were chosen to provide the entry into mortality. Jehovah (Jesus), the Firstborn of the Father, was chosen to play the redemptive role with an infinite and eternal atoning sacrifice of His body and His blood. Thus, with all of this outlined and anticipated in heaven before any spirits had come to mortality, Jesus has been appropriately identified in holy writ as "the lamb slain from the foundation of the world" (Revelation 13:8; Moses 7:47).

This symbolism of the lamb was introduced to the mortal Adam and Eve, who in their temporal state outside the Garden of Eden had forgotten much that had gone before. Adam and Eve and those who followed them were commanded to offer as a similitude of Jesus—the Lamb who would come—an unblemished male lamb, the firstling of the flock, thus keeping before the people a reminder of their need for redemption and the reassurance that the Anointed One would come to provide it (see Moses 5:5–8). When Christ actually did come and offer up that ultimate sacrifice, the symbolic offering required of the generations that would follow was changed to that of a broken heart and a contrite spirit (see 3 Nephi 9:18–22).

JOHN 1:29, 36; 1 PETER 1:19;
REVELATION 5:12; 22:3; 1 NEPHI 10:10; 13:35–41;
DOCTRINE AND COVENANTS 59:8; 76:85; 88:106

LAST

See Alpha and Omega, Beginning and End, First and Last

JACOB 4:16

LAST ADAM

See Adam

LAW

LAWGIVER

The two great governing principles for citizens in the kingdom of God are love and law. Jesus combined those two succinctly when He said, "If ye love me, keep my commandments" (John 14:15). "I am the law," He declared to the Nephites (3 Nephi 15:9), and as such is the perfect lawgiver, giving commandments whose only purpose is to increase our opportunity for happiness and enhance our ability to love.

ISAIAH 33:22; JST, MATTHEW 9:18–19; 3 NEPHI 15:5;

DOCTRINE AND COVENANTS 38:22; 45:59; 64:13

LEADER

In all things Christ is our leader, both by precept and by example. Like David of old, the Son of David would be a victorious "leader and commander" (Isaiah 55:4) of the people. In times of fear or temptation, one of the most reassuring promises to all of us is that the Lord will "lead [us] along" (Doctrine and Covenants 78:18).

PSALM 23:2; DOCTRINE AND COVENANTS 38:33; 112:10

LIFE

WORD OF LIFE
PRINCE OF LIFE

Christ is the Life of the World (John 1:4; Doctrine and Covenants 12:9) and the life of all humankind in it (Doctrine and Covenants 93:9). He provides eternal life spiritually through His atoning forgiveness of sin, and He provides eternal life physically by breaking the bands of death through His Resurrection. Truly He came that in every way we "might have life, and . . . have it more abundantly" (John 10:10).

JOHN 5:26; 6:33; 11:25; ACTS 3:15; 1 JOHN 1:1; 5:11–12; 3 NEPHI 9:18; 11:11; DOCTRINE AND COVENANTS 10:70; 34:2; 39:2; 45:7; 88:13

LIGHT

LIGHT OF THE WORLD

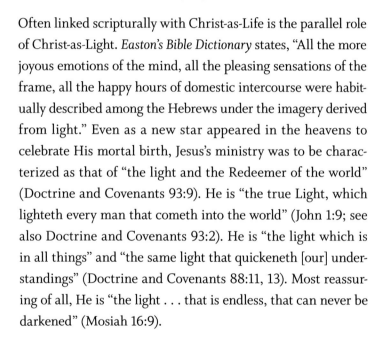

Often linked scripturally with Christ-as-Life is the parallel role of Christ-as-Light. *Easton's Bible Dictionary* states, "All the more joyous emotions of the mind, all the pleasing sensations of the frame, all the happy hours of domestic intercourse were habitually described among the Hebrews under the imagery derived from light." Even as a new star appeared in the heavens to celebrate His mortal birth, Jesus's ministry was to be characterized as that of "the light and the Redeemer of the world" (Doctrine and Covenants 93:9). He is "the true Light, which lighteth every man that cometh into the world" (John 1:9; see also Doctrine and Covenants 93:2). He is "the light which is in all things" and "the same light that quickeneth [our] understandings" (Doctrine and Covenants 88:11, 13). Most reassuring of all, He is "the light . . . that is endless, that can never be darkened" (Mosiah 16:9).

JOHN 1:7–8; 8:12; 12:35; 3 NEPHI 11:11; 15:9; MORONI 7:15–19;
DOCTRINE AND COVENANTS 34:2

Some specific designations regarding
Christ-as-Light include:

Light of Israel

ISAIAH 10:17

Light of Truth

DOCTRINE AND COVENANTS 88:6

Light That Shineth in a Dark Place

2 PETER 1:19; DOCTRINE AND COVENANTS 6:21

Light to Lighten the Gentiles

ISAIAH 42:6; LUKE 2:32

Light, True

DOCTRINE AND COVENANTS 88:50; 93:2

Light unto All Who Sit in Darkness

JST, LUKE 3:7

Light Which Cannot Be Hid

DOCTRINE AND COVENANTS 14:9

Light Which Ye Shall Hold Up

3 NEPHI 18:24

LION OF THE TRIBE OF JUDAH

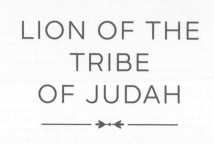

saiah likens Jehovah's determination to fight ferociously in defense of Israel to that of "the lion and the young lion roaring on his prey" (Isaiah 31:4). This is backdrop to John's declaration of Christ as the "Lion of the tribe of Juda," invoking qualities of royalty, majesty, strength, and courage (Revelation 5:5).

Lord

This is one of the most frequently used titles for Jesus in the scriptures, especially when referencing Jehovah in the Old Testament. Its most common synonym is *Master*, suggesting governance and authority over possessions, property, and people, such as a medieval "lord of the manor" or "master of the house." Fortunately, in the case of Christ, His lordly role is characterized by benign, loving governance and authority.

It should be noted that, as with the use of a title such as *God*, *Lord* is often applied to the Father, thus making it sometimes problematic in determining which of these two Deities is being referenced. Obvious examples appear in the Psalms, where David's cries are virtual prayers directed toward the *Lord*. He to whom prayers are directed has traditionally been the Father, not the Son. However, inasmuch as Jehovah serves under the Father in the Old Testament and as such is the God of those people, it is sometimes unclear to whom prayers are being directed in that era.

Many and varied are the uses of *Lord* when referring to Jesus in the scriptures, including but certainly not limited to these:

Lord and Christ

ACTS 2:36

Lord and Savior Jesus Christ

2 PETER 1:11; 3:18; DOCTRINE AND COVENANTS 20:1, 30

Lord and Your Redeemer, Jesus Christ

DOCTRINE AND COVENANTS 15:1

Lord Both of the Dead and Living

ROMANS 14:9

Lord God

JUDE 1:4

Lord God Almighty

REVELATION 15:3; 2 NEPHI 9:46

Lord God of Abraham, Isaac, and Jacob (Israel)

EXODUS 32:27; 1 CHRONICLES 29:10, 18; ALMA 29:11

Lord God of Gods

JOSHUA 22:22

Lord (God) of Hosts, Sabaoth

ISAIAH 47:4; ROMANS 9:29; 1 NEPHI 20:2; 2 NEPHI 8:15; 13:15;
DOCTRINE AND COVENANTS 1:33; 88:2; 95:7

Lord God Omnipotent

REVELATION 19:6; MOSIAH 3:21

Lord, Holy and True

REVELATION 6:10

Lord Jesus

ACTS 7:59; 1 THESSALONIANS 4:1;

MOSIAH 3:12; MORONI 6:6

Lord Jesus Christ Our Saviour

TITUS 1:4

Lord My God, Mine Holy One

HABAKKUK 1:12; JOHN 20:28

Lord of All

ACTS 10:36

Lord of Glory

1 CORINTHIANS 2:8; JAMES 2:1

Lord of Heaven and Earth

ZECHARIAH 6:5; ACTS 17:24; 1 CORINTHIANS 15:47;

DOCTRINE AND COVENANTS 55:1

Lord of Kings

DANIEL 2:47

Lord of Lords

DEUTERONOMY 10:17; 1 TIMOTHY 6:15;

REVELATION 17:14

Lord of Peace

2 THESSALONIANS 3:16

Lord of the Sabbath

MATTHEW 12:8; LUKE 6:5

Lord of the Vineyard

JACOB 5

Lord Omnipotent

MOSIAH 3:5, 17, 18

Lord Our Righteousness

JEREMIAH 23:6

Lord the Judge

JUDGES 11:27

Lord Their God, Thy God, Your God

EXODUS 20:5; JOEL 2:23, 26–27; 3:17;

DOCTRINE AND COVENANTS 98:47

Lord, Their Redeemer, True Messiah

1 NEPHI 10:14

Lord, Your Holy One

ISAIAH 43:15

MAJESTY

This is another term of royalty and authority, linked with *King, Lord,* and *Highness.* It is easy to recognize here the adjectival form of the word: *majestic.* Christ is majestic and will come with that kind of dignity and authority to rule on earth.

DOCTRINE AND COVENANTS 20:16

MAKER

This is a title referring to Christ's role as Creator and Framer of "the heavens and the earth, and all things that in them are" (2 Nephi 2:14; 3 Nephi 9:15). A less obvious but equally true application of this title is not only His power to create but also His power to cause. Thus, He can make things (create them), and He can cause things (make things happen). In their most striking form, these latter events are usually called miracles.

JOB 35:10; ISAIAH 45:9, 11; 2 NEPHI 9:40; ENOS 1:4; MORMON 9:11

MAN

SON OF MAN

See also Son

Most of the meaning of Christ-as-Man comes from His mortal sojourn as opposed to His deified activities before and after mortality. In that sense Pilate (and almost everyone else) did not recognize the significance of his own language when he cried out during Jesus's final day, "Behold the man!" (John 19:5). Furthermore, this title reminds all that Jesus was a man in form and appearance after His Resurrection as well as before it, descending out of heaven to appear to the Nephites as "a Man . . . clothed in a white robe" (3 Nephi 11:8). Inasmuch as Jesus was created in the express image of His Father, this should be a firm reminder of the divine bodily form (that of a man) that characterizes the Father's appearance as well as the Son's. Indeed, one of the Father's principal names is "Man of Holiness" (Moses 6:57), with Christ regularly being called *the Son of Man*. As such, Christ could therefore appropriately be a man of sorrows, could be tempted (although He did not yield), could tire, be hungry, feel sorrow and pain (see Luke 22:44). Perhaps His most praiseworthy achievement in the mortal aspect of His life is suggested by Peter, who boldly declared Him to be "a man approved of God" (Acts 2:22).

ISAIAH 53:3; LUKE 21:36; 22:22; JOHN 6:27; ROMANS 5:15;
1 TIMOTHY 2:5; 1 NEPHI 11:16–26; DOCTRINE AND COVENANTS 65:5

Master

See Lord

MATTHEW 10:24–25; 23:8–10; LUKE 9:33; 18:18;
JOHN 13:13; EPHESIANS 6:9

MEDIATOR

MEDIATOR OF THE NEW COVENANT

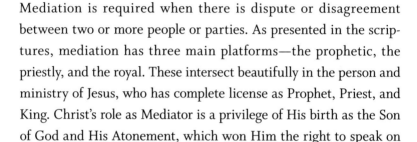

Mediation is required when there is dispute or disagreement between two or more people or parties. As presented in the scriptures, mediation has three main platforms—the prophetic, the priestly, and the royal. These intersect beautifully in the person and ministry of Jesus, who has complete license as Prophet, Priest, and King. Christ's role as Mediator is a privilege of His birth as the Son of God and His Atonement, which won Him the right to speak on behalf of others. Other related roles such as *advocate* and *counsel*, both of which are legal terms, underscore the fact that "cases" will be brought before the bar of eternal justice, and the defendants need representation. Christ is our representative in those proceedings and will seek reconciliation with Heavenly Father on behalf of His mortal children, all of whom have transgressed and lost their own standing before the bar of justice.

1 TIMOTHY 2:5; HEBREWS 8:6; 9:15; 12:24; 2 NEPHI 2:28;

DOCTRINE AND COVENANTS 76:69; 107:19

MESSENGER OF SALVATION

MESSENGER OF THE COVENANT

— ⟩•⟨ —

He spoke the truth because He was the
Truth. The Messenger was the message,
and salvation was the reward.

MALACHI 3:1; 3 NEPHI 24:1;
DOCTRINE AND COVENANTS 93:8

MESSIAH

See also Christ

Jesus identified Himself to the prophet Enoch as "Messiah, the King of Zion, the Rock of Heaven" (Moses 7:53). As such He was *the Anointed One,* a title translated from Hebrew into Greek invariably as *Christos:* He who would save the children of Israel from their enemies and restore to them the promises of their fathers. Internal theological conflict among Jews in the meridian of time could often be traced back to the issue of the long-promised Messiah. Where was He? When would He come? Would God keep His promise to send Him? Of course, He did come, but not with the power and political impact many had anticipated. Consequently, many of His own tribe and heritage did not recognize Him and still wait for that advent. There will yet be an advent with just such power and political impact, but it will be His second appearance on earth, not the first.

DANIEL 9:25; JOHN 1:41; 1 NEPHI 1:19; 10:14, 17;

2 NEPHI 25:19

Minister of the Sanctuary

---　➤·◄　---

This suggests Christ's priestly role in temples, both ancient and modern, and underscores His relationship with saving ordinances generally. His is a "more excellent ministry" (Hebrews 8:6) devoted to those He came to save. We could all do more to revere the time we have worshipping Him in the sanctuary, the sacred space of our buildings.

MATTHEW 20:28; HEBREWS 8:2–3

NAIL IN A SURE PLACE

————— ➤·◄ —————

In a moving Messianic tribute, Isaiah prophesied of Christ's mission and Crucifixion with these words:

"And I will clothe him with thy robe, and strengthen him with thy girdle, and I will commit thy government into his hand: and he shall be a father to the inhabitants of Jerusalem, and to the house of Judah.

"And the key of the house of David will I lay upon his shoulder; so he shall open, and none shall shut; and he shall shut, and none shall open.

"And *I will fasten him as a nail in a sure place*; and he shall be for a glorious throne to his father's house.

"And *they shall hang upon him all the glory of his father's house, the offspring and the issue,* all vessels of small quantity, from the vessels of cups, even to all the vessels of flagons.

"In that day, saith the Lord of hosts, shall the nail that is fastened in the sure place be removed, and be cut down, and fall; and the burden that was upon it shall be cut off: for the Lord hath spoken it" (Isaiah 22:21–25, emphasis added).

When the Roman soldiers drove their four-and-one-half-inch crucifixion spikes into their victim's flesh, they did so first in the open palm. But because the weight of the body might tear that flesh and not sustain the burden to be carried, they also drove nails into the wrist, down in the nexus of bones and sinews that would not tear no matter what the weight. Thus, the nail in the wrist was the "nail in a sure place." Once it was removed and the Savior was "cut down," the burden of the crucified body (more literally, the burden of the Atonement) was brought to an end. In terms of our salvation, Christ is the Nail in a Sure Place—never failing, never faltering, ever the most certain and reliable force in eternity. For this we surely "hang upon him all the glory of his father's house."

OMNIPOTENT

———— ➤·◄ ————

See also Almighty; Power of God

This is most often seen as a characteristic and quality of godhood rather than a title. Nevertheless, it is used as a name seven times in scripture, six of those by King Benjamin or those who heard his magnificent sermon as recorded in the Book of Mosiah. This distinction is another testament to the individuality of authorship among those writing in the Book of Mormon.

REVELATION 19:6; MOSIAH 3:5, 17, 18, 21; 5:2, 15

ONE

———— ➤·◄ ————

This somewhat awkward translation of Zechariah's description regarding the circumstances of the last days declares: "And the Lord shall be king over all the earth: in that day shall there be one Lord, and his name one" (Zechariah 14:9). The Apostle Paul yearned for the day in which there would be "one Lord, one faith, one baptism, one God and Father of all" (Ephesians 4:5–6). Zechariah seems to be prophesying that such unity will come, including a unified understanding that there will be one name and one name only whereby the human family can be saved.

ONLY BEGOTTEN
ONLY BEGOTTEN SON
ONLY BEGOTTEN OF THE FATHER

Jesus, born of Mary, a mortal mother, was fathered by Elohim, an immortal God. As such, He is the only half-divine, half-mortal child in the family of humankind. Exactly how this conception took place has not been revealed. Luke records that Jesus would be called "the Son of the Highest"; the Holy Ghost came upon Mary and "the power of the Highest . . . overshadow[ed]" her. Thus, the baby born of her was "called the Son of God" (Luke 1:32, 35). Nephi quotes the Spirit who was giving him a vision of the future as having said, "Behold, the virgin whom thou seest is the mother of the Son of God, after the manner of the flesh" (1 Nephi 11:18).

JOHN 1:14; 3:16; 2 NEPHI 25:12; JACOB 4:5; ALMA 5:48; 9:26;
DOCTRINE AND COVENANTS 20:21; 93:11; MOSES 1:6, 21; 5:9; 6:57

OUR
PASSOVER

———— ➤•◄ ————

Adam and Eve were instructed to introduce the ordinance of sacrifice by offering the blood of a male, unblemished, firstborn lamb.
The children of Israel enhanced and expanded that symbolism when
they marked the doorposts of their homes with the blood of a lamb,
thus allowing the destroying angel to *pass over* the firstborn sons
who were in those homes. This became the most visible and his-
toric Old Testament prefiguration or type of Christ's Atonement,
wherein His blood allowed all to escape death and hell, or to literally
be *passed over* from the fate of eternal death and confinement. No
other type or prefiguration of Christ can transcend Passover in the
precision of its various elements and the beauty of their meaning.

EXODUS 12:7, 12–13; 1 CORINTHIANS 5:7

Peace

LORD OF PEACE

PRINCE OF PEACE

FOUNDER OF OUR PEACE

———— ➤·◄ ————

Surely among the most oft-quoted and deeply cherished utterances of the Savior are these from the final twenty-four hours of His mortal life: "Peace I leave with you, my peace I give unto you: not as the world giveth, give I unto you. Let not your heart be troubled, neither let it be afraid" (John 14:27). What a remarkable declaration, particularly in light of what He was about to endure in Gethsemane and at Calvary. How beautiful upon the mountain are His feet for His determination to deliver the gift of peace.

ISAIAH 9:6; EPHESIANS 2:14; 2 THESSALONIANS 3:16;

2 NEPHI 19:6; MOSIAH 15:18

PHYSICIAN

———— ➤•◄ ————

Jesus blessed the physical body in two ways. First and foremost, He provided a universal resurrection for all humankind. He also was a healer of mortal bodies not yet deceased. Indeed, it has been observed that His entire earthly ministry consisted of teaching and healing. Matthew records:

"And Jesus went about all Galilee, teaching in their synagogues, and preaching the gospel of the kingdom, and healing all manner of sickness and all manner of disease among the people. . . .

"And they brought unto him all sick people that were taken with diverse diseases and torments, and those which were possessed with devils, and those which were lunatic, and those that had the palsy; and he healed them" (Matthew 4:23–24).

Similarly, during His visit to the Nephites in the Book of Mormon, Jesus said: "Have ye any that are sick among you? Bring them hither. Have ye any that are lame, or blind, or halt, or maimed, or leprous, or that are withered, or that are deaf, or that are afflicted in any manner? Bring them hither and I will heal them" (3 Nephi 17:7).

LUKE 4:23; MOSIAH 3:5; MORONI 8:8

PLANT

TENDER PLANT
PLANT OF RENOWN

— ➤•◄ —

Many of the titles and descriptions of
Jesus suggest a living, organic quality.
He is described, by turns, as a seed, stem,
branch, and vine. Above all He and His
Atonement represent the fruit of the tree
of life, that which was "desirable above all
other fruit" (1 Nephi 8:11–12).

ISAIAH 11:1; 53:2; EZEKIEL 34:29; ZECHARIAH 3:8;
JOHN 15:1; MOSIAH 14:2

Potter

No image or title in scripture carries the message of yielding to Deity more effectively than does the metaphor that Jehovah is the Master Potter and we are the clay He shapes, forms, and fires into beauty.

ISAIAH 64:8; ROMANS 9:20–21

POTENTATE

———— ➤·◄ ————

This title is seldom used in modern times but was very common in some cultures anciently, referring to those who held office as a ruler or monarch. It takes its meaning from the word *power*, drawing upon a common root with other related words such as *potent* and *potential*.

1 TIMOTHY 6:15

POWER OF GOD

———— ➤·◄ ————

Jesus *has* the power of God and *is* the power of God in the sense that He is the Father's agent in almost every task He undertakes. In Their work both He and the Father are omnipotent, meaning They are all-powerful, with unrestricted strength. However, it should be said that their omnipotence is limited to *what can be done,* realizing some things *cannot be done,* such as saving a man "in his sins" as opposed to saving him "from his sins" (see Alma 11:34–37; Helaman 5:10).

EXODUS 32:11; 2 CHRONICLES 20:6; PSALM 66:3; MATTHEW 22:29; LUKE 5:17; 9:43; 22:69; ROMANS 1:16; 1 CORINTHIANS 1:18, 24; DOCTRINE AND COVENANTS 88:13

PRECIOUS

In another application of the theme Christ-as-Stone, the early writers made clear that this particular Stone was active, efficacious, and elect—in a word, precious. Christ and His Atonement were also considered to be the "precious fruit" (1 Nephi 15:36) in Lehi's vision of the tree of life.

1 PETER 2:6

PRINCE

PRINCE OF PEACE
PRINCE OF LIFE
PRINCE OF THE KINGS OF THE EARTH

As a prince is a king-in-waiting, a son tutored under his father to take the latter's place eventually, so Jesus was a *Prince* to Elohim, anticipating the time when He would rise from the prince's position at the Father's feet to stand with Him as rightful heir at His side. It is significant that the title *Prince* is, with only rare exception, linked with *peace,* as if that were to be the chief characteristic and quality of the kingdom of heaven.

ISAIAH 9:6; DANIEL 9:25; ACTS 3:15; 5:31;
REVELATION 1:5; 2 NEPHI 19:6

PRIEST

———➤◄———

CHRIST IS A PRIEST IN THE HIGHEST AND HOLIEST MEANING OF THAT WORD. THE PRIESTHOOD OF GOD BEARS HIS NAME: THE HOLY PRIESTHOOD AFTER THE ORDER OF THE SON OF GOD. HE STANDS AT THE HEAD OF THAT ORDER, IS AUTHORIZED TO USE PRIESTHOOD POWER IN ANY WAY HE SEES FIT, AND IS "A PRIEST FOR EVER" (HEBREWS 7:17), HAVING BEEN ORDAINED TO THAT OFFICE "FROM THE FOUNDATION OF THE WORLD" (ALMA 13:7).

ALMA 13:1–2, 6–10;
DOCTRINE AND COVENANTS 107:3–4

PROPHET

———— ➤·◄ ————

It may seem unusual to call Jesus a *Prophet* inasmuch as we usually think of Him as one who speaks to and guides prophets. Nevertheless, this is a perfectly appropriate designation for Christ, as the word means literally "one who speaks as a guide or leader." At its most elevated application, it is "one who speaks for God." Much more than being simply a foreteller of the future, a prophet is a teacher, a speaker for or leader of a distinct cause, movement, or belief. Christ certainly qualifies as *Prophet* by these standards; indeed, He qualifies more than any of the other leaders to whom that appellation has been given. His own words and deeds testified of His divinity, a principal truth of which any true prophet must ultimately testify.

DEUTERONOMY 18:15; MATTHEW 21:11; LUKE 7:16; 24:19;
JOHN 6:14; 7:40; 1 NEPHI 22:20–21; 3 NEPHI 20:23

PROPITIATION

———— ➤·◄ ————

In the process of satisfying justice and reconciling man to God in matters of sin and transgression, some payment or ransom had to be offered for human errors. A *propitiation* is that appeasement or agreed-upon peace offering, a role only Jesus was pure enough and willing enough to play.

ROMANS 3:25; 1 JOHN 2:2; 4:10

PURIFIER

————— ➤·◄ —————

It is suggested in scripture that when Christ appears in His triumphant final appearance, the most obvious virtue we will recognize in Him may well be His purity. In order that "we [may] be like him" (Moroni 7:48) when He comes, we must seek for that same purity, a blessing ultimately available only through Jesus Himself. Perhaps no other gift coming to us in the great Atonement of Jesus Christ can be more refreshing and encouraging than the gift of being made clean, of being purified. Following his great sermon, King Benjamin heard his audience cry out: "O have mercy, and apply the atoning blood of Christ that we may receive forgiveness of our sins, and our hearts may be purified; for we believe in Jesus Christ, the Son of God" (Mosiah 4:2). That is the cry that should precede baptism and every other sacred ordinance we receive at God's hand.

TITUS 2:14; HEBREWS 9:13–14; 3 NEPHI 19:28

RABBI

RABBONI

———— ➤•◄ ————

The literal Hebraic meaning of this title is actually "master," but its broad and more customary meaning is "teacher." The integration of those two definitions casts valuable light on how important religious knowledge was and is in the Jewish tradition. In virtually no other society is the teacher/scholar in the community also considered to be the true leader in that community. *Rabboni*, uttered by Mary Magdalene in acknowledging the resurrected Christ, is the most honorable of titles for a teacher, meaning "my great master." Her use of this appellation is evidence of how respectful she was of both Christ's teachings and His leadership, and how emotionally laden such a title can be at a very personal level.

JOHN 1:38, 49; 3:2; 6:25; 20:16

REDEEMER

REDEEMER OF ISRAEL

————— ➤·◄ —————

One of the most frequently used titles for Christ, this applies to His triumph in redeeming or "buying back" that which was spent or lost (our physical and spiritual lives). It implies that something that had existed before is now returned to the original owner, as one might redeem a mortgage on a house or a wristwatch that had been pawned. Christ reclaimed our bodies from death and our spirits from hell, paying the ransom, "buying them back" from their lost and fallen circumstance.

1 NEPHI 10:5–6; 20:17; 21:7, 26; 3 NEPHI 9:21; 20:13; MORONI 8:8;

DOCTRINE AND COVENANTS 8:1; 10:70; 15:1; 18:11; 34:1; 93:9; 138:23

REFUGE FROM THE STORM

————— ➤·◄ —————

Whatever our challenges are, whatever troubles may come, whatever pain we feel, or whatever storms arise, Jesus is our refuge and protection in such times. Just as He calmed the Galilean storm when His disciples were sure they were going to lose their lives, so can He calm our storms and give us refuge from them until they dissipate and life is calm again. In such times, He will be "a strength to the needy" and "a shadow from the heat" (Isaiah 25:4).

MARK 4:35–41; HEBREWS 6:18

THE
RESURRECTION

—— >•‹ ——

The reason Christ could provide a Resurrection is because He was the Resurrection. The power to take up His own life after Roman crucifixion had taken it from Him and after His body had lain in a tomb is the mysterious, lifesaving, life-giving, life essence of Divinity. One of the boldest declarations in all of holy writ is Jesus's personal witness to Martha, sister of Lazarus and Mary, that He, Jesus, is "the resurrection and the life," and he or she "that believeth in [him], though he were dead, yet shall he live: and whosoever liveth and believeth in [him] shall never die" (John 11:25–26).

RIGHTEOUS

RIGHTEOUSNESS

This title, uncommon as it is, may well be the perfect one-word label for the Son of God. It is what His beloved Apostle John called Him, and it is what the prophet Enoch called Him—two unique witnesses with special righteous qualities of their own. He is not only Righteousness personified, but He also unfailingly demonstrates that virtue in all of His various assignments and duties.

ISAIAH 53:11; JEREMIAH 23:6; 2 TIMOTHY 4:8;

1 PETER 2:22–23; 1 JOHN 2:1; 2 NEPHI 9:41; 26:9;

DOCTRINE AND COVENANTS 17:9; MOSES 7:47

ROCK

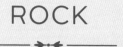

See also Stone

When life is in commotion and nothing seems sure or stable, when people and things are driven about by every wind of doctrine and every wave of society's whims, when nothing seems deep-rooted or solid or permanent, how dearly we need something firm, steadfast, and immovable. How dearly we need a rock to hold on to. Jesus is that Rock and is so labeled repeatedly throughout the scriptures. One of the great declarations in all of holy writ comes from a father telling his sons to build their foundation "upon the rock of our Redeemer, who is Christ, the Son of God, . . . a sure foundation, a foundation whereon if men build they cannot fall" (Helaman 5:12). With one's stance firmly fixed on this mighty rock, the men and women of Christ will be able to honor the commandment to "stand . . . in holy places and be not moved" (Doctrine and Covenants 87:8). Some of the most striking and beautiful imagery in the scriptures has to do with rocks. The Psalms, for example, are replete with the psalmist's cry of appreciation for the "rock of salvation" and the "rock of strength." They are repeatedly seen as a refuge and protection, both literally and figuratively. Of course, to the enemies of righteousness, Christ is a different kind of rock—a "rock of offense" (2 Nephi 18:14) over whom transgressors stumble.

DEUTERONOMY 32:4; PSALMS 31:2–3; 61:2; ROMANS 9:33;

1 CORINTHIANS 10:1–4; 1 PETER 2:8; 1 NEPHI 15:15

Specific applications of this title include:

Rock of Heaven

MOSES 7:53

Rock of Israel

2 SAMUEL 23:3

Rock of Refuge

PSALM 94:22

Rock of Righteousness

2 NEPHI 4:35

Rock of Salvation

2 SAMUEL 22:47; PSALM 89:26; JACOB 7:25

Rock of Strength

PSALM 62:7; ISAIAH 17:10

Root

See David

ISAIAH 53:2; MOSIAH 14:2

RULER

This is yet another title suggesting Christ's reign as king, governor, and magistrate, reminding us of Isaiah's prophecy that "the government shall be upon his shoulder" (Isaiah 9:6). As the agent of His Father, He rules in heaven now, and in the end of time, He will rule on earth.

MICAH 5:2; LUKE 1:33; 1 CORINTHIANS 15:24–25;
1 NEPHI 17:39; 2 NEPHI 29:7;
DOCTRINE AND COVENANTS 41:4; 133:61

SALVATION

See Savior

ISAIAH 62:11; LUKE 19:9–10; 1 NEPHI 13:36

SANCTUARY

In biblical history, the sanctuary of the temple was the most sacred place within it. In the sanctuary, a designated animal was sacrificed and the blood of it offered as part of a ceremonial atonement for the sins of the people. More generally speaking, a sanctuary is any place of refuge or asylum that provides protection, safety, and care for those who retreat there. As an appellation of Christ and His Atonement, perhaps its most revealing designation was that sacred place in any church or holy building where fugitives were entitled to immunity and protection from arrest. Clearly such safety and merciful protection against the demands of justice are personified in Jesus, the Savior and Redeemer of all humankind.

EXODUS 30:10; LEVITICUS 8:15; 16:18, 33; ISAIAH 8:14; EZEKIEL 11:16

SAVIOR

SAVIOR JESUS CHRIST

———— ➤•◄ ————

"For God so loved the world, that he gave his only begotten Son, that whosoever believeth in him should not perish, but have everlasting life. For God sent not his Son into the world to condemn the world; but that the world through him might be saved" (John 3:16–17). These verses are among the most beautiful and moving declarations ever made about the plan God provided for the salvation of His children. They are oft-quoted and much loved by Christians of all sorts and affiliations. It is inspiring each time one hears or reads them, no matter how often that may be.

Unlike *redeem,* which is to buy back, to *save* means to preserve or protect, to deliver one from danger. We all respond to stories of heroism in which a child is saved from a burning home or a soldier is saved from the field of battle. Jesus is that Savior to the entire world, including every man, woman, and child who has lived or ever will live in it. "Beside him there is no Savior" (Doctrine and Covenants 76:1). Some of His saving gifts are unconditional; all receive them regardless of worthiness or merit. Other aspects are conditional, requiring our obedience to principle and acceptance of the gift through covenantal promise. But conditional or unconditional, our future would be doomed if it were not for the saving grace of Jesus, the Son of God, who conquered death and hell for everyone who "believeth on his name and bringeth forth fruit meet for repentance" (Alma 12:15).

ACTS 13:23; PHILIPPIANS 3:20; 1 TIMOTHY 1:15; 4:10;
2 TIMOTHY 1:10; HEBREWS 7:25; 2 PETER 2:20; 3:18;
1 NEPHI 21:6; 2 NEPHI 31:13; 3 NEPHI 5:20;
DOCTRINE AND COVENANTS 19:41; 20:1; MOSES 1:6

Qualifying and clarifying descriptions of
Jesus's role as Savior include:

Saviour, Great God and

TITUS 2:13

Saviour, Just God and

ISAIAH 45:21

Saviour, Prince and

ACTS 5:31

Saviour of the Body

EPHESIANS 5:23

Saviour of the World

JOHN 4:42; 1 JOHN 4:14; 1 NEPHI 10:4;
DOCTRINE AND COVENANTS 43:34

SWEET
SAVOUR

———— ➤·◄ ————

In the Old Testament, Jehovah outlines in some detail how the various offerings called for in the law of Moses were to be made. Never was that more true than of the principal blood and burnt offerings that were in similitude of the Lamb of God, He who would be offered as the ultimate blood sacrifice. When these ancient rites were performed correctly, the smell of the sacrifice (the significance and meaning of it) was "a sweet savour unto the Lord" (Leviticus 1:9).

EPHESIANS 5:2

SECOND MAN

———— ➤·◄ ————

See Adam

1 CORINTHIANS 15:47

SERVANT

RIGHTEOUS SERVANT

In the last evening Jesus would spend with His Apostles, He introduced the ordinance of the sacrament of the Lord's Supper and then knelt to wash the feet of these devoted men who were about to face far more challenges than they could have possibly imagined. As resistant as some were to this humble, self-effacing act, Jesus nevertheless taught, "The servant is not greater than his lord; neither he that is sent greater than he that sent him" (John 13:16). He was giving them the example of the greatest among them being the servant of all, a lesson they were to learn and demonstrate in their own ministries.

ISAIAH 42:1; 53:11; MATTHEW 12:18; 20:27–28;
PHILIPPIANS 2:7; MOSIAH 2:17–19

SHEEP

See Lamb

ISAIAH 53:7

SHEPHERD

GOOD SHEPHERD

———— ➤•◄ ————

It has been said that the most familiar verses of scripture in all of the Old and New Testaments are those in Psalm 23, which begins, "The Lord is my shepherd" (Psalm 23:1). A shepherd knows his sheep, and they know him. He provides good pasture for them and protects them against predators. He knows their names and, if one is missing, he immediately seeks that stray or endangered animal. He leads that wanderer back to safety and, if necessary, he carries the lame or wounded one on his shoulders until it can be healed and healthy again. Jehovah is the Good Shepherd of the Old Testament and Jesus is the Good Shepherd of the New. At some time in life all will feel the need—and be grateful for—the shepherding guidance Christ gives to those who are lost or straying.

GENESIS 49:24; MATTHEW 15:24; 18:12–13;
JOHN 10:11, 14; 1 NEPHI 13:41; ALMA 5:38;
DOCTRINE AND COVENANTS 50:44

Additional emphasis on Jesus as shepherd
is included in these verses:

Shepherd and Bishop of your Souls

1 PETER 2:25

Shepherd, Chief

1 PETER 5:4

Shepherd, Great and True

HEBREWS 13:20; HELAMAN 15:13

Shepherd of Israel

PSALM 80:1

SHILOH

———— ➤•◄ ————

In the book of Genesis, the coming of the Lord is referred to as the coming of "Shiloh" (Genesis 49:10). That reference might be unclear were it not for the Joseph Smith Translation, which offers this interpretation, "Messiah who is called Shilo" (JST, Genesis 50:24). Although the actual meaning of the word Shiloh is debated, we know it was the name given to an ancient city in Samaria, the major Israelite worship center before the building of Solomon's temple. Some linguists think the word means "peace."

SON OF GOD
SON OF MAN

———— ➤·◄ ————

Several of the titles given to the Savior are obvious, and to those who accept the scriptural description of Jesus's birth, *Son* may be the most obvious of all. It is the belief of the faithful that this baby boy born in Bethlehem was the son of Mary, a mortal woman more highly favored by that role than any mother could possibly be favored in any other way. But more singular than the motherhood of a mortal woman was the fatherhood of an immortal, divine, glorified Man—Elohim, God the Eternal Father, the Man of Holiness. In the New Testament Gospels alone, as written by Matthew, Mark, Luke, and John, the title "the Son of Man" appears eighty-three times. Furthermore, throughout all scripture this title for

Jesus is by far the most common. "Son of God," used less often but sometimes with more impact, was so sacrosanct that His claim of that relationship was used against Jesus in the people's condemnation of Him as a blasphemer.

Inasmuch as the Savior's humility is one of the most inspiring aspects of His character, always deferring to His Father's counsel and always obedient to His Father's will, it would seem that the title *Son* perfectly captures both the deference and the dignity that characterized Jesus all of His mortal life. Surely no higher tribute could possibly be paid than to have *this* Father repeatedly say of *this* Offspring, "This is my beloved Son, in whom I am well pleased; hear ye him" (Matthew 17:5).

MATTHEW 3:17; JOHN 5:27; ACTS 3:13;

ROMANS 1:3; 8:32; GALATIANS 2:20; 4:4;

COLOSSIANS 1:13; 1 THESSALONIANS 1:10;

HEBREWS 1:2; 4:14; 10:29; 2 PETER 1:17;

2 NEPHI 31:13; MOSIAH 15:2–8; ETHER 3:14;

DOCTRINE AND COVENANTS 58:65; 76:73; 93:15;

MOSES 6:57; JOSEPH SMITH—HISTORY 1:17

Some of the specific roles as *Son* that Jesus played are:

Son Ahman
DOCTRINE AND COVENANTS 78:20; 95:17

Son of Abraham
MATTHEW 1:1

Son of David
MATTHEW 1:1; 9:27

Son of God Most High
LUKE 8:28

Son of Joseph
LUKE 4:22; JOHN 1:45

Son of Righteousness
3 NEPHI 25:2; ETHER 9:22

Son of the Blessed
MARK 14:61

Son of the Eternal Father
2 JOHN 1:3; 1 NEPHI 11:21

Son of the Highest
LUKE 1:32

Son of the Living God
MATTHEW 16:16; 2 NEPHI 31:16; MORMON 5:14;
DOCTRINE AND COVENANTS 55:2

Son of Thy Bosom
DOCTRINE AND COVENANTS 109:4

SPIRIT OF TRUTH

————— ➤·◄ —————

Referring to an embodied being as a spirit is not common in the scriptures. However, because the body and the spirit constitute the "soul of man" (Doctrine and Covenants 88:15) and because in the Godhead the Father, Son, and Holy Ghost are, except for their physical distinctiveness, completely united, it is certainly appropriate to interchange descriptive appellations given to divine Beings. This is especially true in this instance, inasmuch as it was Jesus Himself who said, "I am the Spirit of truth" (Doctrine and Covenants 93:9, 26).

BRIGHT AND MORNING
STAR

————— ➤·◄ —————

Stars are frequently used as symbols in the gospel of Jesus Christ, not the least incident of which was a new star signaling His birth in Bethlehem. Stars represent light, guidance, hope, and the glory of God's celestial handiwork. John's reference in the book of Revelation to Christ as the "bright and morning star" suggests that He is the last star visible in the heavens before dawn, constantly in place through the dark night. He will stay with us through even our darkest hours and then bring those nights to an end when His role changes to "the Sun of righteousness," with the warmth, radiance, and redemption that title implies.

MALACHI 4:2; REVELATION 22:16

STEM OF JESSE

—— ►◄ ——

See also Branch; David

Jesse was the father of David, he who became
Israel's greatest king. Christ was variously both a
branch and a *stem* in this royal lineage.

ISAIAH 11:1;
DOCTRINE AND COVENANTS 113:1–2

STONE

———— ✦·◀ ————

See also Rock

In a lyrical description of Christ's undergirding strength to all, Isaiah wrote, "Therefore thus saith the Lord God, Behold, I lay in Zion for a foundation a stone, a tried stone, a precious corner stone, a sure foundation" (Isaiah 28:16). Later Peter would call Him "a living stone, . . . chosen of God, and precious" (1 Peter 2:4). In a metaphor that appears one way or another in each of the standard works, Christ is described as a foundational Stone for those who will believe in Him. Indeed, He is the Chief Cornerstone of individual lives, of the true Church, and of the great plan of salvation, the Stone upon which all can build safely.

However, for many He has been and will be not a stone to build upon but one to stumble over, a burdensome impediment that many would-be builders "refused" (Psalm 118:22), "disallowed" (1 Peter 2:4, 7), or "set at nought" (Acts 4:11). To these, Christ would be "a rock of offense" (2 Nephi 18:14). Nevertheless, in the end He is for all humankind "the stone upon which they might build and have safe foundation . . . [the] stone [that] shall become the great, and the last, and the only sure foundation" (Jacob 4:15–16).

GENESIS 49:24; LUKE 20:18; EPHESIANS 2:20;

DOCTRINE AND COVENANTS 50:44

Strength

Christ (Jehovah) is our "everlasting strength"

(Isaiah 26:4). As such He is not only "the Strength

of Israel" (1 Samuel 15:29) but the "strength and . . .

song" (Isaiah 12:2) of each individual.

SUN OF RIGHTEOUSNESS

In the English language it is impossible to resist the word association of "sun" and "Son" as they apply to Jesus. He is the Bright and Morning Star still shining at night, the Day Star and the Dayspring coming brightly with the dawn. As "the sun of righteousness" He is "in the sun, and the light of the sun, and the power thereof by which it was made" (Doctrine and Covenants 88:7). To all who look to Him, He is a "sun and shield" (Psalm 84:11), the Light of the World that will never be darkened.

MALACHI 4:2; MOSIAH 16:9

SUPREME BEING

This is another of the titles that can be equally and appropriately applied to both the Father and the Son. With the resurrected Jesus standing on the right hand of Elohim, these two are united in their glory at the pinnacle of the universe.

ALMA 30:44; DOCTRINE AND COVENANTS 107:4

TABERNACLE OF GOD

———— ✦·◆ ————

A tabernacle is a dwelling place or house of habitation. The more
sacred the purpose of the tabernacle, the more it takes on the significance of a sanctuary. The human body is considered a tabernacle in
which the person's divine spirit dwells. John called Christ the "tabernacle of God," meaning that He is a sanctuary from the world, and
the spiritual power of the Godhead dwells in Him (Revelation 21:3).

TEACHER

———— ✦·◆ ————

See also Rabbi

As honest as he was in his declaration, Nicodemus dramatically
understated the truth when he said of Jesus, "We know that thou art
a teacher come from God" (John 3:2). There are three things necessary for great teaching—a profound message, an inspired and inspiring instructor to deliver it, and an audience eager to hear and learn
from it. Jesus provided the first and second of these requirements in
abundance wherever and whenever He taught. What remained in
question in His time and our own is the third element. "He that hath
ears to hear, let him hear" (Matthew 11:15). Only we can provide
that last ingredient in the teaching and learning formula.

JOB 35:11

THAT
WHICH I HAVE
CHOSEN

———— ➤•◄ ————

It is not often a pronoun becomes a noun, much less a title. But such is the case in the passage from the book of Moses that reads: "And that which I have chosen hath pled before my face. Wherefore, he suffereth for their sins" (Moses 7:39).

THRONE

———— ➤•◄ ————

Isaiah said this of the Lord's future Atonement: "I will fasten him as a nail in a sure place; and he shall be for a glorious throne to his father's house" (Isaiah 22:23). The image of a *glorious throne* is the image of majesty and rulership, which will be the eternal right of the resurrected Christ.

TOWER

———— ⟩•◂ ————

Jesus is a Tower of strength and salvation, rising above and standing preeminently over His people. As a tower is of distinct advantage in seeing an enemy "when he is yet afar off" (Doctrine and Covenants 101:54), so too is Christ an advantage in giving us both protection and a far-reaching view of the plan of salvation. He is a high tower, a strong tower, and ultimately a tower of salvation.

2 SAMUEL 22:3, 51; PSALMS 18:2; 61:3; 144:2;
PROVERBS 18:10

TRUTH

———— ➤·◄ ————

The book of Revelation declares that in the hour of the Apocalypse Jesus will be called *True*. During His mortal life the Savior said of Himself, "I am . . . the truth" (John 14:6). In the simplest of declarations, Jesus was "He that is true" (Revelation 3:7).

REVELATION 19:11

That description is applied in at
least these many ways:

True and Living God
JEREMIAH 10:10; 1 JOHN 5:20;
1 NEPHI 17:30; HELAMAN 13:18

True, Holy and
REVELATION 6:10

True Light
JOHN 1:9;
DOCTRINE AND COVENANTS 88:50; 93:2

True Messiah
2 NEPHI 1:10

True Shepherd
HELAMAN 15:13

True Vine
JOHN 15:1–5; 1 NEPHI 15:15

True Witness
REVELATION 3:14

Truth, Lord God of
PSALM 31:5

Truth of the World
ETHER 4:12

UNCHANGEABLE ONE

———— ➤·◄ ————

The prophets have taught that in order for us to have faith in God and trust in His judgments, He must be consistent. He is. His course is one eternal round. He is the same yesterday, today, and forever. He is unchanging and unchangeable.

1 NEPHI 10:18; 2 NEPHI 27:23; MORMON 9:19; MORONI 10:19;

DOCTRINE AND COVENANTS 20:17

VINE

———— ➤·◄ ————

One of the most poignant scriptural images of our relationship to Christ is the beautiful, organic analogy of precious fruit growing from the life-giving influence of vine to branch to blossom, all watched over and nurtured by a loving, attentive gardener. "I am the true vine, and my Father is the husbandman," Jesus taught His disciples, "[and] ye are the branches: He that abideth in me, and I in him, the same bringeth forth much fruit: for without me ye can do nothing" (John 15:1, 5).

1 NEPHI 15:15

WAY

WAY OF SALVATION
A MORE EXCELLENT WAY
NEW AND LIVING WAY

The journey toward exaltation is frequently likened to walking a path. Nephi's great concluding testimony described repentance and baptism as the "gate by which [one enters the] . . . strait and narrow path" (2 Nephi 31:17–18). If we press forward faithfully on that path and endure to the end place to which it leads, we will have eternal life. "This is the way; and there is none other way," Nephi concluded (2 Nephi 31:21). Christ knew that same doctrine of salvation regarding His mission in life when He said, "I am the way" (John 14:6)—in short, *that* way Nephi referred to, besides which there is no other. He is the "way of salvation" (Acts 16:17) and one whom the writer of Hebrews called a "new and living way" (Hebrews 10:20).

MATTHEW 7:14; 2 NEPHI 31:17–21; ETHER 12:11

WELL BELOVED

In one of the movingly powerful but seldom-cited miracles of the Book of Mormon, the later Nephi and Lehi are imprisoned and threatened with the loss of their lives. Into that setting the Holy Spirit comes and the voice of the Father whispers, "Peace, peace be unto you, because of your faith in my Well Beloved, who was from the foundation of the world" (Helaman 5:47).

WITNESS

Often when we think of those whose ministry it is to bear witness of the gospel of Jesus Christ, we fail to remember that He too is a witness of the same truths—a "faithful and true witness" (Revelation 3:14). He said of Himself, "To this end was I born, and for this cause came I into the world, that I should bear witness unto the truth" (John 18:37).

ISAIAH 55:4; REVELATION 1:5

WONDERFUL

————— ➤·◄ —————

That title originated by the prophet Isaiah (with the help of the scholars who translated the King James Bible) to celebrate in prophecy the birth of the baby Jesus means literally that which astonishes, fills with surprise, or at which one marvels. We experience all of that and more when we feel the wonder of Christ's role in our salvation.

ISAIAH 9:6; 2 NEPHI 19:6

WORD

————— ➤·◄ —————

"The apostle whom Jesus loved"—John the Apostle—was able to use words very skillfully in describing the Word. Indeed, perhaps it was because of his literary duties that John seems particularly taken with this title for his Lord and Master. In the introduction of the Gospel that bears his name, John wrote: "In the beginning was the Word, and the Word was with God, and the Word was God. The same was in the beginning with God. . . . And the Word was made flesh, and dwelt among us" (John 1:1–2, 14). This metaphor for Jesus was expanded in John's epistles, wherein he wrote, "Our hands have handled . . . the Word of life" (1 John 1:1) and "there are three that bear record in heaven, the Father, the Word, and the Holy Ghost" (1 John 5:7).

John the Baptist appears to have used the title of *Word* for the Savior before any other did so (see JST, John 1:15–16; Doctrine and Covenants 93:6–18). It is instructive that Christ Himself used words as His principal tool in His role as "the Word, even the messenger of salvation" (Doctrine and Covenants 93:8). Even the Father acknowledged this distinctive element of the Savior's ministry when He referred to Jesus as "the word of my power" (Hebrews 1:3).

JST, JOHN 1:14; REVELATION 19:13;

DOCTRINE AND COVENANTS 29:30; MOSES 1:32

EPILOGUE

Perhaps in a book devoted to the names and titles of Christ it is appropriate that the final entry be *the Word*. I have filled a number of pages with many words in an effort to sketch even the briefest dimensions of Jesus Christ's mission and majesty. But ultimately words fail us, and, in that sense, I have failed the Word. No matter how much we write or how many titles we apply, mortal man and the human vocabulary will never do justice to Him whose impact and power, whose importance and presence, are "clear as the moon, and fair as the sun, and terrible as an army with banners" (Doctrine and Covenants 5:14; 105:31). I have loved writing about this greatest of all men; nevertheless, I admit failing in my effort to capture on paper the proper respect and admiration that should be given the living Son of the living God. Even if I were better at using them, there aren't words precise enough, or grand enough, or plentiful enough to praise adequately the Redeemer of our souls. As the frustrated Ammon said, so say I: "I cannot say the smallest part which I feel" (Alma 26:16). But what I feel is worth everything I possess. After all the titles and testimonies noted here are tallied up, "this is the testimony, last of all, which we give of him: That he lives!" (Doctrine and Covenants 76:22). It is an unmerited, unanticipated, and unspeakable privilege to be a witness for His names.

ACKNOWLEDGMENTS

In seeing this little project through to completion, I am indebted to many—both in The Church of Jesus Christ of Latter-day Saints and those of other faiths—who have written on this subject. It has been a topic of great interest for centuries, and I have benefited by reviewing the work of many who wrote well before the days of computers and word-search capabilities. I have included a very brief bibliography listing a handful of these sources for those readers who may want to delve deeper into this rewarding subject.

As always, I thank my friends at Deseret Book Company for their interest in, encouragement for, and professional preparation of this manuscript. As with virtually every book I have ever written, this did not start out to be a book. Like most of the others, this was intended to be a personal study project for me and my family. But our friend of many years, Sister Sheri Dew, somehow heard of such a study project. Before I knew it, we were talking about graphic design and manuscript deadlines. Pat and I are grateful to Sheri for her friendship, her devotion to the kingdom, and her impact on Deseret Book Company. In addition to Sheri, I wish to express appreciation for Emily Watts's always keen editorial touch and buoyant disposition. Both have been needed. I thank Laurel Day for her oversight of the project and Sheryl Dickert Smith and Richard Erickson for their remarkable creative work on the book's design. Given the unusual nature of the text, including the many variations of a single title in some cases, I felt I handed them an impossible graphic challenge. I could not have been more pleased with their ordering and designing of the contents.

I am particularly indebted to Janice Stringham LeFevre for her assistance with this project. Janice is as gifted in her research and technical capability as anyone with whom I have worked over the years. To say she was prodigious in her research and documentation would be a severe understatement; it was clear from the outset that Janice could not do anything by halves.

I am also grateful to my wonderfully able executive assistant and secretary, Lisa Beth Atkin. Lisa lives daily with the impossibility of my calendar but was somehow able to block out time for me to work on this book—even if that turned out to be primarily holidays, airplane travel, and late nights. In addition to all else she does to manage the complexity of my apostolic life and duties, she gave valuable insight and editorial advice during preparation of the endless drafts it takes for me to write anything. I am totally dependent on Lisa's exceptional managerial skills for the smooth running of a very busy office.

Finally and always, I express thanks to my beloved wife, Pat, to whom the book is dedicated. Due to a cryptogenic illness that struck her down at the very time I was starting to do more with this book, there was every possibility—indeed, every probability—that she would not survive, and I would be left to fulfill the remainder of my apostolic calling alone. Knowing I could never do that, the Lord fulfilled in my behalf what is perhaps His most oft-repeated scriptural promise—"Ask, and it shall be given you." He restored her to my side just short of the full dimension of the miracle that restored Lazarus to his sisters Mary and Martha. I realize it is not always His will that such a miracle be performed, and others have made similar pleas that were not answered as they hoped. For some grand and unknown reason, I was granted this most urgent of all supplications. In a very real sense, this book has its most precious meaning for me in that frightening experience we had together while I was writing it.

As with every private piece of writing I have ever undertaken, I alone am responsible for any doctrinal errors or inaccurate commentary that may appear in this book. I realize how difficult it is for a lay reader to separate my personal expressions from the official declarations of The Church of Jesus Christ of Latter-day Saints or the Quorum of the Twelve Apostles of which I am a member, but separate them you must. Not the First Presidency of the Church, the Quorum of the Twelve Apostles, The Church of Jesus Christ of Latter-day Saints, nor Deseret Book Company are in any way responsible for the content and opinions expressed in this book. I hope these pages are error-free to every reader and inspiring to at least a few of those readers, but if neither of these hopes is realized, it is my fault and mine alone.

SELECTED BIBLIOGRAPHY

Albright, William Foxwell, and David Noel Freedman. *The Anchor Bible,* vol. 27, *Mark: A New Translation and Commentary.* Edited by C.S. Mann. New York: Doubleday, 1986.

Baker's Evangelical Dictionary of Biblical Theology. Edited by Walter A. Elwell. Grand Rapids, MI: Baker Books, 1996.

Bible Dictionary. In Latter-day Saint edition of the King James Version of the Bible. Salt Lake City: The Church of Jesus Christ of Latter-day Saints, 2013.

ChurchofJesusChrist.org (website). Produced by The Church of Jesus Christ of Latter-day Saints. 2019. https://churchofjesuschrist.org.

The Complete Joseph Smith Translation of the New Testament: A Side-by-Side Comparison with the King James Version. Edited by Thomas A. Wayment. Salt Lake City: Deseret Book, 2005.

Derk, Francis H. *Names and Titles of Christ.* Minneapolis: Bethany Fellowship, Inc., 1969.

Easton, M.G. *Illustrated Bible Dictionary.* New York: 1893.

Gaskill, Alonzo L. *The Lost Language of Symbolism: An Essential Guide for Recognizing and Interpreting Symbols of the Gospel.* Salt Lake City: Deseret Book, 2003.

Hitchcock, Roswell D. *Hitchcock's Bible Names Dictionary.* New York: A.J. Johnson and Sons, 1878.

Holland, Jeffrey R. *Christ and the New Covenant.* Salt Lake City: Deseret Book, 1997.

Horton, T. C., and Charles E. Hurlburt. *Names of Christ.* Edited by James S. Bell Jr. Chicago: Moody Press, 1994.

International Standard Bible Encyclopaedia. Chicago, IL: The Howard-Severance Company, 1915.

LeFevre, Janice Stringham. "I Am the Nail: Exploring a Metaphor for Christ." Unpublished manuscript, last modified December 2017. Pages for Mac.

Linford, Richard. "Jesus Christ is The Son, Jehovah, The Messiah, the Living Christ, the Savior of the World." Unpublished manuscript.

McConkie, Joseph Fielding. *Gospel Symbolism.* Salt Lake City: Deseret Book, 1985.

McConkie, Joseph Fielding, and Donald W. Parry. *A Guide to Scriptural Symbols.* Salt Lake City: Bookcraft, 1990.

Meeks, Wayne A., et al. *The HarperCollins Study Bible: New Revised Standard Version.* New York: HarperCollins, 1993.

Millet, Robert L. "A Different Jesus? The Christ of the Restoration." In *Jesus Christ: Son of God, Savior.* Edited by Paul H. Peterson, Gary L. Hatch, and Laura D. Card. Provo, Utah: Religious Studies Center, Brigham Young University, 2002.

Oaks, Dallin H. *His Holy Name.* Salt Lake City: Bookcraft, 1998.

———."Taking upon Us the Name of Jesus Christ." *Ensign,* May 1985.

Smith, William. *Smith's Bible Dictionary.* Philadelphia, PA: A.J. Holman & Co., 1901.

Stone, Nathan J. *The Names of God in the Old Testament.* Chicago, IL: Moody Press, 1944.

Talmage, James E. *Jesus the Christ.* Salt Lake City: Deseret Book, 1915.

Vine, W.E. *Vine's Expository Dictionary of New Testament Words.* Minneapolis, MN: Bethany House Publishers, 1984.

Welch, John W., and John F. Hall. "Names and Titles of Christ." Chart 8-16 in *Charting the New Testament.* Provo, Utah: Foundation for Ancient Research and Mormon Studies, 2002. https://byustudies.byu.edu /new-testament-charts.